LEGENDS

FROM THE

FROSTY SONS OF THUNDER

Pennsylvania

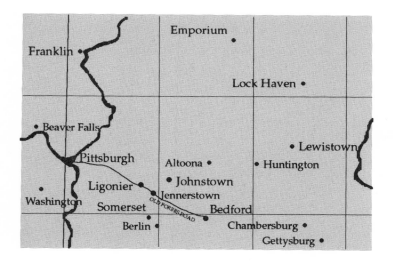

LEGENDS

FROM THE

FROSTY SONS OF THUNDER

To Olg —
With warm personal regards.

William Trall Doncaster, Jr.

William Trall Doncaster Jr.

BRANDYLANE PUBLISHERS, INC.

White Stone, Virginia

✳ Brandylane Publishers, Inc.

P.O. Box 261, White Stone, Virginia 22578
(804) 435-6900 or 1 800 553-6922; e-mail: brandy@crosslink.net

Library of Congress Cataloging-in-Publication Data

Doncaster, William Trall, 1918–
    Legends from the frosty sons of thunder / William Trall Doncaster, Jr.
      p.   cm.
    Includes bibliographical references
    ISBN 1-883911-25-7
    1. Somerset County (Pa.)—History—Ancedotes. 2. Johnstown (Pa.)—History—
Anecdotes. 3. Floods—Pennsylvania—Johnstown—Anecdotes. 7. Nicely, David,
19th cent.—Anecdotes. I. Title.
F157.S6D66 1998
974.8'79—dc21
                                               98–30765
                                                CIP

To my beloved wife,
Marjorie Walker Doncaster

I love thee with the breath,
Smiles, tears, of all my life!— and, if God choose,
I shall but love thee better after death.

"Sonnets from the Portuguese"
Elizabeth Barrett Browning

CONTENTS

Contents

PREFACE

The narrative contained in this volume is a somewhat personal one. It was the result of a privileged conversation with one of America's most revered authors and the fact that I was a professor in the history department of the University of Pittsburgh at Johnstown and living in Somerset, Pennsylvania, at the time. It was the winter of 1968. Then president, Dr. Theodore Bindle summoned me to his office. He had an assignment for me. David McCullough, author of *The Johnstown Flood*, was to be a guest lecturer. Would I host Mr. McCullough while he was a guest of the college? What an assignment! The only difficult part was trying to conceal my exuberant delight. I had admired Mr. McCullough both as an historian and as an author, but never in my wildest imagination had I expected to have the opportunity of meeting him.

In the course of our conversation at dinner the evening of his arrival, I asked Mr. McCullough how he happened to become interested in the Johnstown flood. I was surprised to learn that while he was doing research at the Library of Congress on another subject, he came upon original prints of the Johnstown flood by a photographer from Pittsburgh who, with all his heavy gear and glass plates and the like, somehow managed to get over the mountains and into Johnstown within days of the calamity. He suddenly realized that no one recently had made a definitive study of the subject. At some point in our conversation, somewhat starry-eyed and certainly awed by the presence of the person who sat across from me, I happened to make the statement:

"Mr. McCullough, if only once I could be as absorbed in an interesting study as you have been in the Johnstown flood."

His answer opened the door that fulfilled my desire for challenging research. "You are from Somerset," he said, "and you are sitting on a gold mine. Have you heard of the Nicely brothers?"

In his research on the Johnstown flood, Dr. McCullough had come upon newspaper accounts of the murder trial of Joseph and David Nicely. The brothers were being tried for the murder of a Somerset County farmer, Herman Umberger. The trial occurred simultaneously with the Johnstown flood. Shortly thereafter, as a result of Mr. McCullough's suggestion, I began research on the controversial trial and the unique and quixotic lives of Joseph and David Nicely. During my years of study, I presented many lectures on the subject. I soon

ix

discovered that though their story was remote and more than a hundred years old, it remained not only Somerset County's most remembered history but also had become its most enduring legend.

However, as my research continued, I came upon other lives and legends previously researched by other scholars and by no means exhaustive in mine. My purpose in including them is that I felt they were personalities worthy of the memory of their legend as well as that of the Nicely brothers. A liberty is taken with Jeremiah Black, Frederich Goeb and President William McKinley. My feeling was that their association with Somerset included legendary materials as significant as that of the Nicely brothers. In some cases there is more material than I had originally intended.

Rural Americans during this period lived in a pre-entertainment era when working days were long with back bending toil with little time for recreation. But they were storytellers. When the sun went down and they relaxed before open fires, they shared stories. They liked their heroes to be big, larger-than-life, and capable of accomplishing the impossible. The country in which they lived was wild, wide and open with mighty rivers, rolling plains, towering mountains, and giant forests. Their heroes had to master these challenges, so one like Paul Bunyan came into being. He may have been an early lumberman and stories about him grew large in legend. He was America's own. In like manner, little legends about little people from out-of-the-way-places became larger-than-life within their particular locale.

Most legends are in effect historical accounts, even though people in the actual telling and hearing of them may be unaware that the basic historical facts are being embroidered. Somerset County gave birth to its own legends, its own Paul Bunyan in miniature. They include the legends of Mountain Jack; David "Robber" Lewis; the tragic and ill-fated Frenchman, Noel Huel; and the locally celebrated Joseph and David Nicely.

There are several different versions, particularly of the Nicely brothers legend, that have been passed down through family oral traditions. As with all stories, the storyteller often stretched the truth a little in the telling of the tale. Each storyteller gave the story his own interpretation. Actually there should be nothing strange about different versions of the same legend. As the years go by, storytellers inadvertently make changes in the old tales as they pass them along.

With this in mind, I have attempted to document as much material as possible in order to retain the original version of the legend of the Nicely brothers. My culminating conclusion, as the result of my research, is a somewhat altered and revised version of the brothers tale than that of earlier accounts.

Many of us have heard a lot of folklore in our lives but we were not aware it was folklore. The little that came to me came from my childhood. One of the first legends I recall was that of a headless horseman who visited a place called Sleepy Hollow. My maternal grandfather, Squire Elmer N. Miller, was a country funeral director who lived in Stahlstown, Pennsylvania. On family trips to visit with him and my grandmother, once we left Ligonier, we traveled on a dirt road. The trip seemed endless to my brother and me. To occupy our restless minds, my father would both amuse and frighten us with tales of a headless horseman. It was even more fearful if we were driving on the road at night. The story, of course, was an adaptation from Washington Irving's *Legend of Sleepy Hollow,* but my father made it so real to us that as I grew older it took me a long while to dismiss the headless horseman of Washington Irving from my mind, and to realize that Sleepy Hollow was not near Stahlstown, Pennsylvania, but a place near Tarrytown, New York.

Outworn myths and legends became my fascination, and the legend that involved the Nicely brothers, became my story. To this day, it is difficult to comprehend why this particular legend became so popular in Somerset County, considering a past history of people and occurrences that appeared to be so much more adventuresome and worthy of preservation. Yet the Nicely brothers story has its own fascination set in the context of backwoods superstitions and old farm mystique. Their affair must be considered in the context of the time in which it was enacted; with a national tendency to romanticize the antihero and make him larger-than-life. This particular incident was played out in a small Pennsylvania county by extremely naive and amateur players. Its significance lay in the aftermath of the trial and its consequences, which were simultaneous with the aftermath and consequences of the Johnstown flood. Both became matters of national concern and interest. Both emblazoned the town in the valley and the village in the mountains with deep scars, unforgettable memories, and troubling questions that continue to keep each legend alive.

I began my career as a Presbyterian minister in the mid-1940s in

New Alexandria, a rural town in southwestern Pennsylvania. New Alexandria had been made popular at the time by a novel entitled *The Rolling Years* written by a native of the town, Agnes Sligh Turnbull. I served a congregation of mostly prosperous and retired farmers. An elderly couple in the congregation had adopted a son who was then in his mid-thirties. Unfortunately, the young man was somewhat mentally impaired and a direct target of much of the base humor and idle gossip in the town. His actions became proverbial. Making an afternoon pastoral call on the couple, inevitably the subject of Frankie came up. Wanting to be kind, I strained at words that would be truthful but generous. Frankie's mother was in no way to be fooled. Quick to sense my struggle, she was the one who proved to be both truthful and kind. I can still see the smile on her face and the beginning of a tear in her eye as she proudly said, "Well, Frankie is our boy!" That said it all.

If I may be bold to speak of Somerset's "Frosty Sons of Thunder," I might proudly add, "Well, they are our stories."

I wish to acknowledge my gratitude to Mr. McCullough for introducing me to the legend of the Nicely brothers that made possible this book and my sincere thanks to my publisher, Robert H. Pruett and his associates of Brandylane Publishers, Inc. I want to recall with deepest love and gratitude, my late wife, Marjorie Walker Doncaster, for her devotion and patience as we traveled to many libraries and faraway places with strange sounding names to gather information for this book. I also express my appreciation to my daughter and son-in-law, Debra and Samuel Bruce, for their encouragement and their help in bringing the study to a conclusion; to Margaret Metz Ogle for her time and encouragement in reading the manuscript; to George and John Nicely, a grandson and a great grandson of the Nicely brothers, for their support and interest; and to Dr. Robert W. Matson, my successor at the University of Pittsburgh at Johnstown, and Jeff O'Brien, my friend, for just "being there" when I needed them.

PROLOGUE

From Olympus to the Alleghenies

In Thomas Bulfinch's classic, *Bulfinch's Mythology*, the author writes in the preface, "Mythology is the handmaiden of literature; and literature is one of the best allies of virtue and promoters of happiness." Historically speaking, in every age heroes arise from our hopes of and desires for greatness. Though their aesthetic ideals may be beyond our grasp, their stories become our "best allies of virtue and promoters of happiness." Mythologists show us that adventures of extraordinary humans developed at all levels and in all part so the world. In ancient times and faraway places, wonderful stories are included in numerous religious writings, as the great heroic friendship of David and Jonathan from the Hebrew Scriptures or the delightful Gilgamesh epic from Babylonian mythology, which extols the journeys and friendships of Gilgamesh in his search for immortality. These are stories of men whose courageous spirits and daring adventures became memorable in abiding legends that have endured for centuries.

For many of us, Greek myths first captivated our imaginations with their larger than life characters. Hercules, son of Zeus, was the strongest and one of the most celebrated heroes in classical mythology. His imaginary pillars straddled the Straits of Gibraltar adding allure and grandeur to the Atlantic entrance into the Mediterranean Sea. In the Middle Ages, England's King Arthur and the Knights of the Round Table spurred school children to gallant moral victories and pre-television ideals. Adventuresome stories of the elusive but captivating character known as Robin Hood spanned oceans and centuries. Ballads

1

dating from the fourteenth century extol this dark rebel who, with his companions, stole from the rich and gave to the poor. However, Robin Hood's exploits were not fodder for morality plays or examples of virtuous living. In creating a legend he robbed and killed representatives of the king. The legend, in time, downgraded the robbery and killing and the forest revels of Robin Hood crossed the Atlantic and laid something of a foundation for young America's cowboy and Indian legends. In the New World's primitive beginnings are to be found the seeds of Mount Olympian deeds and Robin Hood's graces that would be superimposed on another type of hero. His heritage would be European, but his image would be forged on an American wilderness anvil.

In like manner such heroic Greek gods were once believed to have lived their lives on Mount Olympus. As children, their heroic plights became our dreams of greatness. But in time our nation grew, Mount Olympus faded for a more local history, spawned with characters more rustic than the Olympian gods, more relevant to a wilderness people than the grandeurs of Olympian spheres. Our history, in these chapters, is concerned with the adventures of local characters who never attained the allure of Olympian greatness, but whom time had made local heroes from the lesser heights of the Allegheny Mountains in southwestern Pennsylvania. Despite past history, best know and best remembered is the legend of Joseph and David Nicely. As their story unfolds, they will be remembered as "the best allies of virtue and promoters of happiness"; anti-heroes though they purport to be.

An American Flavor

The earliest legends and myths to be found in the new world were those held by the American Indian. In time they would be passed on to early pioneers through oral tradition. Of particular interest to this study are the legends and myths of the Iroquois Nation, which include tales about animals, witches, and good and evil spirits, all entwined with devout spiritual beliefs. To the animistic Native Americans, real powers dwelled in mountains, rivers and rocks. The objects were "enmeshed in the web of the universe, pulsating with life and potent with medicine" (Endors and Ortz 1984, XI). Iroquois folklore must have been known, at least fragmentarily, to early scouts and settlers through association with friendly Indians. Though there is little evidence to establish any kind of permanent residency in Somerset County, the Allegheny Mountains of southwestern Pennsylvania were selected by the Iroquois as a hunting ground. The Iroquois Nation possessed a visible material culture; a chain reflected in a body of folklore that has survived. When legends endure, they endure fiercely. "Men still carry oddly shaped pebbles, bits of flint, a piece of fossil agate, in their medicine bundles. We still have legends of rivers, lakes, waterfalls and mountains, the abodes of spirits who often appear as living characters in stories" (Endors and Ortz 1984, XI). As these survive in our pioneer culture so endures the Iroquois legend of their most intriguing hero, known as Hiawatha.

On American soil, to Olympian myth and Arthurian legend, we now add the towering figure of Hiawatha. He would become one of those typically American heroes who possessed exceptional characteristics of strength, determination and cleverness. As interpreted by Indian and American mythmakers, such heroes could overcome obstacles, save themselves from disaster, and outwit the most villainous of villains.

As the new nation gradually came into being, particular charismatic characters came into their own in a new America exclusive of Native American origins. They came from "ranks of leaders, explorers, pioneers, soldiers and statesmen to inspire love of or teach the ethics of success" (Botkin 1983, 2). They were ordinary local people who, in changing times, would share their status in the nineteenth century with a popular and growing breed of another nature "the gentleman on horseback and the demon with the six shooter" (2). Most of these newly made heroes were known only in limited circles or in obscure rural areas, little touched by professional writers. "They might well be the most original, distinctive, characteristic, and certainly, the most abounding collection of folk heroes to emerge in this country" (Coffin and Cohen 1978, xxviii). For the most part their reputations were regional and somewhat off the beaten path, but they served the needs of isolated folk communities.

There were a few notable exceptions. The back bending work that awaited our pioneer ancestors as they carved out a life in the wilderness at times seemed impossible to endure. Such harsh conditions demanded larger than life heroes who could survive almost anything. Despite the unique territorial origins of America's legendary characters, some were taken over nationally, out of necessity,. Yet in the process, such characters almost surely were distorted to fit a wider purpose. Paul Bunyan illustrates this point. His stories were born of fragmentary references to workers in the logging industry. "He had to grow into doing the impossible to fulfill the visions and complete the dreams of westward expanding country" (Coffin and Cohen 1978, xxviii-xxix). Early Americans amused themselves in fireside story and tall tales by visualizing Paul Bunyan and Babe, the Big Blue Ox, doing the ridiculously impossible as a matter of course. "The backwoodsmen" were the first of our 'tall men,' whose words became 'tall talk' and whose deeds were the inevitable 'tall tales' (Botkin 1983, 3). In pursuit of game, skins, land, or adventure the backwoodsman followed the shifting fringe of settlement. He presented the "dwindling of the hero from the godlike or kinglike to the average human level." There was Pennsylvania's Daniel Boone, the great scout and Indian fighter whose Herculean prowess swung him across rivers on the tangling tough fibers of wild grape vines; a restless pioneer who pushed westward through the Kentucky wilderness. Davy Crockett, the "Coonskin Congressman," from Tennessee, could ride the sun around the world and get off where he pleased. He kept a piece of sunrise in his pocket and rode his pet alligator up the waters of Niagara Falls (Botkin, 3). Other tales developed about other widely known characters, not for their good deeds, but for their disreputable crimes. Blackbeard's cruel actions and rich booty made his type of piracy the subject of many stories told particularly along the coasts of the Carolinas. People of the far West took pleasure in retelling the story of the young outlaw and desperado, Billy the Kid. Their lives all grew into legends that were larger than life exaggerations.

Along with these infamous national figures, countless local characters developed. Though genuine personalities, they were known only to people from a small geographical or rural area. Many times the stories were embroidered in the retelling. Some were early settlers renowned for their pranks rather than their skills. Some were eccentrics, like Mountain Jack, who wandered the countryside. Not always heroes in the heroic sense, they gave to people living in isolated parts of America a sense of local identity and pride in their individuality and experiences. Localization prevented Americans from being overwhelmed by the immensity of the land by rooting them to a particular part of the past and allowing themselves to bring forth their own folklore, as Joseph and David Nicely became legend.

Some of the legends in this book embody elements of the foregoing patterns. They are concerned with certain nineteenth century personalities which are regional, have been made over into tall tales that are larger than life. All are in some way associated with that section of the Old Forbes Military Road that runs through Somerset County, Pennsylvania.

Gentlemen on Horseback and Demons With Six Shooters

Nineteenth century murderers and robbers were not, as some historians might lead us to believe, always inventions from metropolitan areas. In many cases, they were the products of frontier towns. As a backlash of the Civil War, poverty, and the lack of vocational opportunity, veterans and the young unemployed experienced a discontent that often led to crime. They became restless spirits beguiled into the daring world of the outlaw. The desire for adventure and excitement often were forces more motivating than the sinister acts of robbery and murder.

Such backwoods desperadoes were not without their more illustrious prototypes. Early on the morning of August 21, 1863, as the Civil War entered its last and most bitter phase, a pale-eyed criminal led a company of bearded horsemen, bristling with weapons, down a mountain ravine into the sleepy little town of Lawrence, Kansas. All participants wore low-crowned, broad-rimmed hats. Most were stoop shouldered, without coats, wearing red flannel shirts. At their head rode a svelte, self-assured outlaw making a fine figure on horseback. Magnificently mounted, he wore a soft black hat with a yellow gold cord, a shirt ornamented with fine needle work and cavalry boots. He was William Clarke Quantrill and his followers were known as Quantrill's Guerrillas (Coffin and Cohen 1978, 162; cf. Andrews 1962, 783).

The peace of the slumbering town was broken by a holocaust of flames kindled by the picturesque raiders. The celebrated Lawrence Massacre, unlike the sacking of other cities during the Civil War, had no real military purpose. It resulted in an orgy of blood and destruction because of a hunger amounting to avarice and notoriety on the part of one man, Quantrill (Coffin and Cohen 1978, 162; cf. Andrews 1962, 783).

There is a peculiar link between the crimes of Quantrill and the Somerset robbery and murder allegedly performed by Joseph and

David Nicely. Bizarre as it may seem, the brothers were lineal successors, not by blood, but by a long line of personal connections, from Quantrill through two other infamous murderers and bandits, Jesse and Frank James, to whom the Nicely brothers claimed relationship. The succession made a veritable dynasty of outlaws.

While neither excuse nor justification can be made for the Lawrence Massacre in which 142 persons lost their lives, it is a matter of historical significance to reflect on the remarks of Major John N. Edwards, Quantrill's chief apologist. An officer of the Confederate Army and well-known Kansas City editor, Edwards wrote in the *Times*, May 12, 1872:

> Quantrill may be likened to a blood Apollo of the prairies. His eyes were very blue, soft and winning. Looking on his face we might say there is the face of a student. If there is a race born without fear, Quantrill belonged to it. In his war-life which was one long merciless crusade, he exhibited all the qualities of cunning, skill, nerve, daring, physical endurance, remorseless cruelty, abounding humor, insatiable revenge and a courage that was sometimes cautious to excess and often desperate to temerity (Coffin and Cohen 1978, 162).

The passage illustrates the curious deification of figures in border outlawry. To Major Edwards, Quantrill was an exciting prairie adventurer, yet his "eyes very blue, soft and winning" hardly accord with the general impression of his victims. Quantrill was a maniacal, fanatical killer whose motives were evil. Yet in keeping with the times, the more notorious outlaws were heroes and heroes were revered.

In like fashion, other aspiring desperadoes took to their independent ways. New faces appeared. One was a young man with striking features, the same steel blue eyes; yet so reckless that even his closest companions stood in dreadful awe of him. He was the infamous Jesse Woodson James. Never hesitating to kill, legend has gilded him with a patina of romance. James was looked upon as a combination Robin Hood and frontier adventurer. The surviving legends about him are for the most part generous and hero-worshiping. Starting his career with Quantrill's bushwhackers, he became in the fifteen years following the Civil War the most notorious train and bank robber in the country. A price of $10,000 was placed on his head by the Governor of Missouri. Robert Ford, a member of James's gang, was tempted by the reward and killed James in St. Joseph, Missouri, on April 4, 1882. James was hanging a picture in the front room of his house with the doorway open to the street. Rather than attract the attention of passersby with his weapons, he removed both pistols and placed them on a chair while he stood on the bed to fix the picture. Robert Ford had never seen James off his guard before, and seized the opportunity to kill his companion from behind. James heard the click of Ford's pistol as he cocked it and turned to receive the pistol ball over his eye. Ford, fearing the revenge of James's friends, left Missouri for Colorado. There he was shot to death one night by Ed Kelly, a friend of James (Emrich 1972, 301).

Like James, some outlaws were men of great daring and courage. On the other hand, many were savage brutes who killed when there was no need for killing. Most were ignorant men without a trace of education; criminals whom everyone believed deserved their fate (Botkin 1983, 2). Yet a taste for romanticizing their lives and reading about them is almost universal.

On a much smaller scale of dash and notoriety, the example of Quantrill and James spread eastward into rural areas like Somerset County. Nineteenth century travelers frequently were stopped and robbed along the Old Forbes Military Road.

Farmers routinely were terrorized and robbed by mounted armed gangs. Robberies of a similar nature during and after the Nicely brothers robbery and murder of Herman Umberger only fueled the fire of guilt for the Nicely brothers. The brothers lacked the surly élan of their more accomplished and better-known predecessors. Joseph and David Nicely were unpolished amateurs with a raw backwoods naiveté in crime.

Such legends developed as romanticized outlawry. Jesse James epitomizes the image of the "revered outlaw" which endures in legend up to the present time. The phrase "gentlemen on horseback and the demon with a six shooter" portrays the outlaw's necessary ingredients and common characteristics. He is "always kind hearted, generous to the poor, chivalrous to the ladies, driven to outlawry by accident or forces beyond his control; betrayed by one close to him and dead before his time" (Botkin 1983, 286). James's killing and betrayal at the hand of a traitor "was all that was needed to set the seal on the legend. It is one of the necessary and stock ingredients" (301).

7

Legend takes us from the larger than life to the sub-human antihero, from Mount Olympus and King Arthur, through Quantrill and Jesse James, to Somerset's Joseph and David Nicely. Their legend has endowed them with a hero's mantle of sorts, but the Nicely brothers did not rise so high in a make-believe saddle. They were young Ligonier valley farmers, caught in the wild fury of the times, untutored in the ways of the outlaw, and perhaps misjudged by a public for whom justice must be served. Their trial for the murder of Herman Umberger began on the same devastating day as the Johnstown flood.

LEGENDS

FROM THE

FROSTY SONS OF THUNDER

PART ONE

The Southwestern Pennsylvania Landscape

The Town in the Valley

Except for the plot set aside for the unknown dead, the newly erected Grandview Cemetery was sparsely occupied. Laid out on high ground, the securely interred bodies were a good distance, some 700 feet, above the dismembered heart of the city below. Purposefully selected as an extra precaution to the sacred memory of the honored dead, the recently buried were hallowed in the belief that they would be safe from the annual spring floods.

The cemetery had been aptly named. Panoramic perspective afforded a "grand view." In the distance rose the spreading grandeur of the foothills of the sprawling Allegheny Mountains. Densely forested, the rolling mounds held clustered varieties of virgin hemlocks, white pine, giant oaks, and an abundance of sugar maple trees. Soothing vistas of far-viewed, wind-swept waves of mountain greens would momentarily relieve grieving thoughts and ghostly shades that lingered in the valley below. From dark ravines and bellied deepness 777 bodies had been lifted, to be newly buried in the Grandview Cemetery.

Despite the natural beauty and awesome allure of the surrounding Alleghenies, Johnstown, Pennsylvania, was not an attractive town in 1889. Some seventy miles east of Pittsburgh and named for an early emigrant, Joseph Johns, the settlement lay flat, clinging closely to a dark gorge at the convergence of two small rivers. The late nineteenth century mill town emerged as a colorless rounded hollow in the ground.

By the 1880s, the narrow valley town had grown into a business-industrial section at the headwaters of the Conemaugh River.

Notwithstanding its ungainly character, it quickly gained a reputation for being a bustling "iron town." Like Pittsburgh, it had matured along the confluence of the two rivers, but on a much smaller scale. Smoke continuously rose like heavy, blue-gray clouds from the chimneys of iron and steel mills. Acrid odors from seething factories and shrill noises from passing trains were constant smells and sounds that never left the valley. Tongues of flames emerged as furnace doors opened, giving the night sky an eerie red black cast. Diverse national and racial groups that emigrated into the valley cauldron had not melted together easily. Each clung to separate identities, upholding customs and traditions brought from roots in the "old country." The valley's diverse people found survival in an alien and strange land. Johnstown became a place of vague forms of day and dancing fires of night. But most of all there were the stark memories of a fatal flood that would forever mark the low, pluvial, ill-fated town.

There was nothing to distinguish Johnstown from any other mill town in southwestern Pennsylvania in the latter part of the nineteenth century. It did, however, boast that it had been the terminus for a portage railroad; a series of incline planes whereby canal barges on the state-owned Pennsylvania canal system were transported on railway cars over the Allegheny Mountains. But with the coming of main railroad arteries, the unique portage railroad ended its useful days and passed into local history, leaving the leaded valley town with no significant landmarks. So it would have remained had it not been for the disastrous, dramatic occurrence of May 31, 1889, which catapulted the town into national prominence.

Johnstown blazed across the front pages of the nation's newspapers for one overpowering episode. Few news stories before or since were to have such an impact on the American public. Coerced into its unpretentious history were massive, late spring rains that caused the impaired breast of a major upstream reservoir to break, driving a great wall of water some seventy feet high and an estimated 20 million tons of water through the narrow river valley. Virtually everything that had been built over some eighty years was instantly destroyed. The notoriously inadequate, much protested and bitterly resented dam some twelve miles to the northeast had given way during one of the worst rainstorms that had ever been recorded for western Pennsylvania.

Reports of the neglected and shoddily maintained dam had been heard many times in the past and were as many times ignored. The dam provided a mountain lake and summer playground for a small colony of wealthy Pittsburghers, known as the South Fork Fishing and Hunting Club. Organized some ten years previously, the members owned the dam and about 160 acres besides. Sixteen dwellings, called "cottages," had been built along the shore. As the local residents knew, they were far too substantial and pretentious to be referred to as cottages. Even they were dwarfed by the club house which had forty-seven guest rooms and a dining room that could serve 150 people. But most remembered and discussed were the handsome and smooth gliding sailboats; a rare sight to the less privileged settlers in the valley. Consequently, in the flood's aftermath, there developed a derisive "Johnstown attitude" about the dam. Precarious at best, the breast of the dam supposedly had been checked and declared perfectly solid. Skeptics and the Johnstown people knew otherwise. A growing contempt for the "sailboat people," like a deadly poison, spread in the minds of the Johnstown people (McCullough 1968, 39–44).

After personal investigations a verdict was issued confirming what everyone already knew, "death by violence due to the flood caused by the breaking of the dam of the South Fork Reservoir." Newspapers informed the public that the breastwork contained no masonry nor had there been any engineering worthy of the name. The dam was simply "a gigantic heap of earth dumped across the course of a mountain stream between two low hills." Grandview Cemetery and its plot of unknown dead would remain a constant reminder that "what struck was not the retributive hand of Providence" as many ministers declared in subsequent sermons. "Our misery," claimed one of the townsmen, "is the work of man" (McCullough 1968, 253).

Stories of the 1889 flood lived throughout the twentieth century. Everyone who in some way experienced it would remember the circumstances of his own life when the water came. Despite the appalling notoriety the flood brought to Johnstown, the number of persons who lost their lives, and the personal tragedies that would play havoc in hundreds of families for years to come, heroic ventures abounded. The person most tearfully remembered and honorably sainted would be Clara Barton (McCullough 1968, 43, 229–231). Working with her associates around the clock, she remained five months. She left Johnstown with many gifts and blessings and received glowing editorials for her heroic work. Yet there remained sinister speculation of another kind. Most conspicuous were the rogues who preyed on the sympathies of others, particularly in neighboring towns. After taking in all the details, they described as their own heart-rending experiences horror stories which reaped an assortment of lucrative handouts. Some surviving families attempted to disguise the fact that relatives listed among the unfound dead were very much alive in some faraway place. Such surmises seemed well justified when, eleven years later in the summer of 1900, a Leroy Temple showed up to confess he had not died in the flood but had been living quite happily in Beverly, Massachusetts. The morning after the flood he had crawled from the wreckage and lost himself on the other side of the valley (McCullough 1968, 229).

The Morley Dog became the flood's most persistent myth. The ornamental metal dog had been purchased in Philadelphia in 1870 by a local industrialist, James Morley, and placed in the front of the Morley home at Main and Walnut streets. Found down river after the flood, it was resurrected and restored to a small park in the center of town. Although officially it commemorates nothing, the years have brought a certain dignity to the dog, and it has become a symbol of endurance of little known men and women who lived and died in Johnstown.[1]

The Village in the Mountains

Tales of the Morley Dog and other references to Johnstown's greatest tragedy would pale into insignificance and become obscured by a bizarre incident that took place in a mountain village near industrial Johnstown. The village was among the last to be made aware of the May 31 deluge. The South Fork Dam lay to the northeast of Johnstown. Some twenty-five miles due south of Johnstown, nestled snugly in the Allegheny foothills, perched the tiny mountain village of Somerset. Here, the very day of the Johnstown flood, a court trial for two notorious brothers would bring thousands to the county seat and unravel a legend that would captivate the small community as the flood had inundated the town and minds of the people of Johnstown. During the trial, every hotel and lodging house in Somerset was filled to overflowing. The curious from near and far lined the streets. The celebrated occasion would mesmerize the village natives and linger as ballad and folk tale through the next century. Like the Morley Dog, the legend of the Nicely brothers would become Somerset's most persistent myth. As with the Johnstown flood, natives would remember later where they had been and what they had been doing the day the Nicely brothers were hanged.

The curious event was in sharp contrast to the ravages of the flood that brought Johnstown into national and historical prominence. Somerset was rural, its people less diverse in ethnic origin than true of Johnstown. Otherwise secluded and gently peaceful, the village was nestled high in the mountains some 2200 feet above sea level. It was first known as Brunnerstown until it became a county seat on April 17, 1795. An act of the General Assembly was passed for organizing the part of Bedford County west of the Allegheny Mountains into a new county (Cassady 1932, 70–71). Early English settlers named it for Britain's Somersetshire. The county is situated in a unique section of Pennsylvania that is not quite a valley, nor a basin, but a high tableland cupped between the crests of the Allegheny Mountains and the Laurel Ridge. It abounds in glades, wet level lands above the headwaters of numerous streams. Characterized by wild and beautiful scenery, it is associated with cool summers, short growing seasons, and early snows followed by long bitter winters. Each spring the densely forested hills and valleys come alive with newly bonneted leaves. Fields and underbrush become dotted with myriad wildflowers; honeysuckle, arbutus, Dutchmen's britches, and in very remote places, the ever exotic lady-slippers. Great expanses of vibrant colors blanket the countryside in the fall. Outlying forests become deep and darkly covered with dead needles from the stately virgin hemlock. Giant white pines and ghostlike birches solemnly interlace with great patches of mountain laurel and rhododendron. Maples, chestnuts and towering oaks are added in some areas to the lush and varied landscape. Great springs of sparkling mountain water gush forth from every hillside forming beautiful mountain streams. But for the Baltimore and Ohio Railroad, which linked the village with Johnstown, and the breathtaking beauty of the rolling hills that brought visiting nature lovers, Somerset's isolation in 1889 would have been complete.

Early pioneers had found the countryside as formidable as it was awesome. Viewed from the heights of the Alleghenies, some ten or so miles away, vast expanses of open land lay surrounded by dense forested ranges. Harmon Husband, one of the first settlers, recorded his impressions. Writing before the Revolutionary War, he observed:

Nothing could exceed these plains in beauty and luxuriance when vegetation was at its full growth. In many places, for acres, grass was as high as a man, of a bluish color, with a feathery head of thick purple (Cassady 1932, 16).

Somerset in no way resembled the industrial town of Johnstown located in the valley. In 1889, Somerset was a quiet, sleepy little bird's nest of a place. If there could be a comparison, it had to be that both town and village were embedded in thick forested foothills, outstretched like low tentacles from the Allegheny Mountains. There the similarity ended. The village and the town had little in common. After the flood, Johnstown marched toward the end of the century with giant industrial steps. A county seat, Somerset emerged quietly and slowly through the triple earnings of mining, dairy farming and lumbering.

Joseph and David Nicely, brothers from nearby Ligonier, would put the little country seat in newspaper headlines across the country. In a curious way, their names would add uniqueness and a bizarre folklore to the otherwise peaceful mountain village. The infamous crime of the brothers would overshadow other significant events in the county's history. In many respects, the legend of the Nicely brothers is Somerset County. It is, and will remain, Somerset's most enduring history turned legend.

Although lacking in the popularity of the legend of the Nicely brothers, is significant folklore dating even before the founding of the county or the village. It begins with the story of a road and evolving legends associated with that road. It is a road that began possibly as a buffalo trail over which was blazed an Indian trail. Through its mountain passes marched the British General John Forbes and his armies as they created a military road for the purpose of capturing the strategic Fort Duquesne and defeating the French. It later was to become the Pennsylvania Road that brought the Conestoga wagon and pioneering people over the Alleghenies to the headwaters of the Ohio River, the Gateway to the West. Still closely paralleling the old Indian trail, it is now known as the Lincoln Highway, Route 30. A significant portion of this road crossed Somerset County, and by its presence developed a local folklore with strong links to a larger history. This was the land that gave birth to a stalwart people who came to be known as the "Frosty Sons of Thunder."

The title was attributed to Alexander Ogle, Sr., who was to become one of the county's most revered personalties. A general of the Pennsylvania militia, he settled in the county about the time of its formation. Records testify that almost immediately he sprang into prominence. A man of commanding presence and great force of character, he became the county's earliest and most influential citizen, easily identified by his red vest and ruffled shirt. Entering public life, Ogle was eight times a representative from the county in the Assembly and at least one time its representative in the Senate. He also was once a member of Congress. In one of his legislative speeches during the presidency of Martin Van Buren, Ogle designated his constituency "the Frosty Sons of Thunder." The name makes reference to the high altitude of the mountain country; frost being an attribute of thunder. As a figure of speech, Olympus is translated as the Alleghenies and Zeus forges his thunderbolts from the icy fastness of Mt. Davis. The appellation was promptly adopted; a rather forceful and proud name for the citizens of the little mountain county seat. Time would prove the sobriquet to hold and to be an appropriate description of the people (cf. Robinson 1953, I:2).

Somerset Passageways

From a Buffalo Trail

The first thoroughfares were merely traces that had been made by buffalo in seasonal migration quests for feeding grounds. Many routes instinctively followed watersheds and the crests of ridges to avoid summer quagmires and winter snowdrifts. It has been reasonably established that in some parts of America during the pre-Columbian period, as well as afterward, the buffalo was a pioneer in road building. While Pennsylvania was heavily wooded, the undergrowth in the forests was not thick and passage among the trees was relatively open. Appalachian mountain trails were among the first used by pioneer traders and early settlers for transportation as they traveled either by foot or on horseback. Subsequently, when the Indians established lines of communication they laid down primary trade routes between their more prominent villages and courses to hunting grounds, many of which may have followed old buffalo trails (Cassady 1932, 23).

In the 1750s, the shortest distance between Atlantic seaboard settlements and the headwaters of the Ohio River was by way of two Indian trails which crossed the future Somerset County. Few, if any, white men lived permanently west of the Allegheny Mountains at the time. Nemacolin's trail, blazed by an old Indian chief, crossed the southwestern part of the county.[2] It was opened as a military road by General Edward Braddock in 1755. General Braddock had been sent by the British to defeat the French by capturing Fort Duquesne, which was strategically located where the Monongahela merged with the Allegheny to form the Ohio River. Both France and Britain vied for complete control of all lands east of the Mississippi River, with specific focus on the headwaters of the Ohio. Forts were built by the contending nations to protect their claims. Assisted by the young American, Colonel George Washington from Virginia, the ill-fated enterprise ended with the death of General Braddock and Washington's well-known defeat at Fort Necessity. Unsuccessful though it was, the event gave the county a place in history and two distinguished names as a part of that history.

Christopher Gist was one of the first known pioneers to cross the Susquehanna River at Harper's Ferry and head into the wilderness of the West. A surveyor from North Carolina in the employ of the Ohio Land Company, Gist was probably the first white man to enter the unknown Somerset territory. Choosing the southern Nemacolin Trail, his survey was one of the first official charted routes (Doyle 1945, 18). Having blazed a white man's trail across the mountain barriers, he set out the following year to search for another route. On Monday, November 5, 1750, Gist and his party reached the top of the Allegheny Mountains, recording distances between various points. He spent four days in actual travel between the summits of the Allegheny and Laurel Ridge (19).

The Old Forbes Military Road

The Alleghenies, the largest of Pennsylvania's seven mountains, is a part of the greater Appalachian Range, a dramatic mountain landscape that stretches in unbroken line from Newfoundland to central Alabama, a distance of some fifteen hundred miles. Few white men had ventured into the western lands beyond the Alleghenies much before the mid-eighteenth century. When the curtain closed on the historic drama that gave the North American continent to the English instead of the French, the most strategic event was the capture of the French Fort Duquesne. Braddock's humiliating debacle brought about many months of bitter suffering on the frontier. The scalping knife and tomahawk pursued the hardy settlers fleeing for their lives over the Alleghenies. Even regions as far east as the Susquehanna and the town of Lancaster, Pennsylvania, felt the cruel hand of the savages (Rial 1954, 58). To secure British control, into a largely uninhabited territory came the competent British Brigadier General John Forbes. The chronically ill but charismatic general was charged with the task of accomplishing what General Braddock had been unable to do—defeat the French with the capture of Fort Duquesne.

Forbes, a native Scotsman, had been educated as a physician. Choosing instead the life of a soldier, he had risen by rank in the British army. In contrast to the self-willed and aristocratically arrogant Braddock, Forbes was frank and unaffected. From the time of his arrival, colonial authorities were impressed with his character and military prowess. Well-liked by his own soldiers, Forbes gained provincial as well as military respect. Unlike the majority of ostentatious English officers, he had a straightforward manner and a keen intellect. Gathering his army at Philadelphia, Forbes proudly awaited the arrival of his battalion of colorful, kilt-wearing Scottish Highlanders (Shoemaker and McVey 1954, 58).

When Forbes arrived in America, he was made an invalid by an mysterious and ultimately fatal illness. Until mid-September of 1758, he conducted his campaign by voluminous letter writing. In such an urgent circumstance, Colonel Henry Bouquet, an accomplished officer of the Royal Americans, proved to be Forbes's brilliant and shrewd associate. The seemingly impossible military operation through a seemingly impassable mountain terrain became an invaluable training course for the young Colonel George Washington. When General Forbes was able to join his forces, he was incapable of riding a horse and had to be carried in a litter throughout the campaign. This in no way compromised his tremendous ability. The Iroquois, Indian allies of the British, quick to recognize his noble character, called him "Head of Iron" (Rial 1954, 58).

Confronted with the same obstacles that plagued Braddock, Forbes was astounded at the complacency and incompetency of American soldiers and the orders given them by boorish colonial officers. He evaluated them as "an extremely bad lot of broken down innkeepers, horse jockeys and Indian traders" (Rial, 59). Against inconceivable odds, he had a core of 1400 men cutting and clearing a road with as many soldiers deployed in the woods to protect them. He brought together and advanced a military force composed of almost seven thousand men (Echert 1969, 498). General Forbes' military road was constructed over a wagon-trail, previously opened in 1754 by Colonel James Burd from Shippensburg, through Bedford to the top of the Allegheny Ridge. Farther west, the general built a new road (Shank 1966, 16). Colonel Bouquet directed the arduous training of the provincial volunteers and adopted the tactics of the regulars to conditions of wilderness fighting. Bouquet was most influential in convincing Forbes to cut a wagon-wide swath over the Indian trail (Federal Communicative Commission Job Core 1962, 365).

Forbes made the astute decision to press forward toward Fort Duquesne in stages. The most difficult and hazardous part of his expedition was clearing the road to make it wide enough for wagons to travel over the Allegheny Mountains and through the virgin forest. The most challenging stretch of the route would be the fifty miles from Raystown (Bedford) to Loyalhanna (Ligonier). The road would have to cross the hazardous Allegheny and Laurel Mountains, with dark glades in between called the "Shades of Death." The far-reaching objective was a road that would tie the Atlantic settlements together which were furnishing horses, wagons, and supplies for the recapture of British claims beyond the Allegheny Mountains. The road would be guarded by military forts constructed at strategic points (Doyle 1945, 27). In the summer of 1758, eighteen years before the American Revolutionary War, one of the greatest road building works and military efforts of frontier history began. Original plans called for the opening of a road to converge with the wagon road previously opened by Colonel Burd that led to the top of the eastern slope of the Allegheny Ridge. The task had not been completed when news arrived of Braddock's defeat. Under Forbes's orders and Bouquet's direction, the crude road some twelve feet wide was hewn out of the darkness of an oblique mountain wilderness.

As the year wore on, triumph for the British became evident. With the assistance of the devout Moravian missionary, Christian Frederick Post, a superior position was assured. Post had been engaged by the

British to take messages to the Indians in the Fort Duquesne area in the hope of revealing to the Indians the spurious intrigues of the French. Under the profound influence of Post, the Indian allies of the French gradually melted away, weakening the French garrison (Rial 1954, 61). On November 25, 1758, the French abandoned and burned their fort, leaving it for Forbes's forces to occupy. The fort was renamed for William Pitt, the English prime minister.

The road to victory had been an arduous one. Forbes's army steadily and relentlessly penetrated the wilderness. His mission fulfilled, the general was carried back to Philadelphia. Worn and emaciated, Forbes died on March 11, 1759. His acute mastery of the wilderness meant the fall of French power in the Ohio valley. Due to the gravity of his illness, most of the responsibility of Forbes's campaign continually fell to Henry Bouquet. History has granted Bouquet his rightful place in this wilderness victory, particularly in his outstanding valor at the Battle of Bushy Run.[3] Yet not to be forgotten was the striking guidance and superior leadership of General John Forbes in the battle for Fort Duquesne.

When General Forbes issued orders to clear a trail through the wilderness, he not only brought about a great British victory but added an event in history that would be of significance to Somerset County and the opening of the West. The Northern Indian Trail thereafter would be known as the Forbes Military Road, or the Great Road. The military road effectively tied Atlantic settlements beyond the Allegheny Mountains to British claims. It extended from Fort Bedford, the last outpost of colonial culture, to the heart of the wilderness and the Gateway to the West at the forks of the Ohio. Along this road, by evening firelight and log cabin reverie, varying legends would grow and be preserved.

New Roads for the Endless Mountains

By the early 1800s, Forbes Military Road gradually became generally known as the Pennsylvania Road. The first state-sponsored action for such a road began after the Revolution, when Hugh Henry Brackenridge spearheaded a movement to obtain state aid for improvement of east-west transportation in Pennsylvania. As a result of these efforts, the Pennsylvania legislation, in the spring of 1784, authorized a lottery to raise $42,000 for the road improvement (Shank 1988, 20-21). It later became Route 30. It remained the shortest route from Philadelphia to Pittsburgh. The trip required almost a month, depending on weather conditions. Also known as the Great Road or the State Road, despite its steep assents and oppressive road conditions, it was still much preferred to Braddock's Military Road or the National Road.

By the turn of the century the covered wagon had almost completely replaced the packhorse train relied upon by early settlers. Prior settlers and armies of the French and Indian War had relied intensively on the packhorse train. With the advent of settlers in the West the train developed into a business. The packhorse train was usually composed of twelve or more horses with two men in attendance (Buck and Buck 1927, 230). As the road improved, the era of packhorse trains was brought to an end. Early pioneers first made the trip on foot. Usually, the man went first, selected his land, cleared it, planted a first crop in preparation for his family, built his cabin and then returned for his wife and children.

By 1790 there were enough settlers that wagons for transportation became necessary. Such demands brought into being the first crude, springless, stage wagons or coaches. The first stage service from Philadelphia across the Alleghenies to Pittsburgh was established in 1804. The trip was made in six to seven days, the rate being $20.00 per passenger and twenty pounds of baggage. Daily stage coach travel usually began at 3:00 A.M. At better taverns, before departure, ladies fortified themselves with strong coffee and gentlemen with something stronger. Later refinements were made including the hanging of the coach on leather straps that improved the quality of riding. The vehicles were called "stage coaches" because the journey was made in stages between horse changes (Buck and Buck 1973, 26). Conditions remained primitive and uncomfortable. As late as 1817, travelers frequently found it more comfortable to walk over the rough roads, and sometimes stage coach passengers were required to walk uphill in order to lighten the load.

Along with the stage coach was the distinctly American Conestoga wagon (Buck and Buck, 37). Built in Pennsylvania's Conestoga Valley, from which it received its name, this massive four-wheeled covered wagon was crafted by German wagon makers. Strongly built, it measured approximately twenty-six feet long, eleven feet high and weighed some 3,000 pounds. Its bed was shaped and built like a boat and covered with a large cloth top. Since there were no bridges and rivers had to be forded, these boatlike bottoms not only protected the cargo from water damage, but actually floated across the streams like a boat. Traveling slowly, covering ten to fifteen miles a day, they customarily were painted red, white and blue and they were usually drawn by four, six or eight horses (*The Berlin Record* 1932, 13 December; cf. Cassady 1932, 62–63).

In time, the great covered wagon trains became a common sight as they traveled over the Pennsylvania Road. The familiar silhouette became almost synonymous with the western movement. The men who drove the wagons were a race apart, a special legend in themselves, like the breed of horses they drove. Known to be a dashing, roisterous group of rugged individualists, they competed ruthlessly for the business of the road and the right-of-way. Teamsters traveling in opposite directions settled disputes with their fists over the high middle of the narrow roads. A more friendly gesture was associated with the set of bells attached to a special yoke on the collar of a lead horse. Tradition indicates that the bells were surrendered when the rig broke down or literally was "stuck in the mud" to any traveling wagoner who pulled it out. Each driver held the earnest hope that he would reach his destination without the need of assistance or to surrender his bells, that is to say, "I'll be there with bells on" (Lathrop 1935, 142).

After 1812, when the great western migration began, thousands upon thousands of wagons were built for pioneers headed into the new territories. The stage wagon or coach followed closely on the heels of the covered wagon as a carrier. It was a lighter vehicle used mostly for carrying passengers and mail. The stage coach was pulled by four to six horses, and was made to travel rapidly between stations, some ten to fifteen miles apart. At each station a change of horses was made and passengers could acquire refreshments.

An early development along the Pennsylvania Road was the appearance of taverns or inns. During the colonial period Pennsylvania had more inns than any other state. Certain typical features made them easily recognized. Later built of stone, they were seldom more than two stories in height, with an attic window in the gable-ends. Most often the house was almost square, with perhaps an ell in the rear. Invariably across the front was a long porch from which two doors opened; one into the barroom, the other into a hall that opened into the inn parlor or family living quarters (Lathrop 1935, 142).

Every inn had its own characteristics. Differentiation in the patronage of inns depended upon and developed along social standing and reputation. A gentleman alighting from a stage coach rarely slept under the same roof with the wagoner. "Stage stands" catered to stage coach travelers and were at the top of the social ladder. They were separated from the "wagon stands" that were patronized only by the wagoners who slept on bags of hay or oats spread on the taproom floor. Still lower in social standing were "drove stands" for the accommodation of drovers. These had lots into which livestock could be turned and fed. The lowest was the "tap-house," income from which was derived mainly from the sale of liquor. Despite the emphasis on class differences, the bar usually attracted all social classes who would mingle, including the local loafers and drunks. Gossips also gathered at the taverns, which were to become clearinghouses of information, misinformation and rumor. Within these tap-rooms there were circulated many stories of robbery and eerie strangers (Lathrop 1935, 142).

Signboards were a distinguishing feature of all inns. Often they carried no name but merely a significant pictorial device, such as "Green Tree Inn," "Sheaf of Wheat," "Spread Eagle," and "St. George and the Dragon." Since many travelers could not read, they stopped at an inn having a certain sign. One of the earliest and most familiar of the stage stops along the Pennsylvania Road was the "Black Horse Inn," first owned and operated by Casper Stotler. Stotler built a cabin as early as 1762 on the western slope of the Allegheny Mountains. He provided supplies and accommodations for many travelers. Stotler later built a tavern which was popular until the time of the building of the Pennsylvania Turnpike (Baldwin 1964, 36-37).

The first murder committed within the boundaries of Somerset County took place along the Pennsylvania Road and because of it the Black Horse Inn received its name. There are several versions to the story. The following appears to be the most plausible. David Pollock, a young doctor on his way west and riding a black horse, was supposedly shot and killed by one of two traveling Frenchmen. Sometime later, a saddled stray horse was found and taken to the cabin inn. The horse was recognized as belonging to Pollock and the Frenchmen were accused of the murder. Noel Hugel, one of the

Frenchmen accused, was the first person executed in Somerset County for murder. His companion, in an attempt to escape, was mortally wounded. A myth arose of a riderless black horse that could be seen galloping over the road and vanishing at the spot where its owner was murdered, thus giving Casper Stotler's inn the name, the Black Horse Inn (Baldwin 1964, 57).

Some four miles west of Bedford, the Pennsylvania Road was intersected by what came to be known as the "Old Glade Road" (Coleman 1941, 5). Here in 1772, several young engineers were employed to map out an alternative route that would prove to be a shorter and more direct way to the headwaters of the Ohio River. At the fork of the road stood an old tavern known as Bonnets, still a noted landmark (11). Both the Old Forbes Military Road and the Glade Road, were to become notable highways to the Ohio River. The Glade Road seems to have been preferred by travelers to the one through Ligonier, except in wet weather. By 1830, the alternate route was widely known (5) and considered superior to any other for wagons and carriages. It was the least oppressive route over the formidable Allegheny and Laurel Mountains. The road to Pittsburgh via Somerset and Washington, Pennsylvania, could be traveled with more ease and comfort than any other road across the mountains, with access to good inns and taverns.

An interesting sidelight on the Glade Road is the person and background of John Badollet. His journals provide the earliest accounts of this road, so named because it passed through "the Glades" of Somerset County. Badollet was born in Geneva, Switzerland in 1757, four years before the birth of his lifelong friend and better-known Pennsylvania pioneer, Albert Gallatin. As fellow students, they were impressed by the American struggle for independence and the opportunities the new nation might offer. Gallatin arrived in America in 1780, and in 1785 settled at "Friendship Hill" in Fayette County in southwestern Pennsylvania. Within a year Badollet joined him. Badollet's journals mention that the Glade Road branched off from the Great Road to Pittsburgh a few miles west of Bedford. As well as providing an alternate route to Pittsburgh, the road provided access to the Glades country that so appealed to Badollet (Hunter 1982, CIV).

The Glade Road derived its name from the meadowland lying between the Allegheny and Laurel Mountains at the headwaters of Stoney Creek, Laurel Creek and the Casselman River (Coleman 1941, 3).

A summary from Badollet's journal mentions that the Glades have a much colder climate and inferior soil to that located in other parts of the country. However, he saw in the lives of the people of the region a constant industry that resulted in wealth and happiness. His journal touches on a number of topics about the countryside, but his most vivid account is revealed in his fascination with the Glades. He almost regretted that he and Gallatin did not settle in this particular area (Hunter 1982, 37).

At the top of the Allegheny Mountains on the Glade Road stood the White Horse Tavern. It was the best known and most popular of all the inns. Usually thronged with guests, it early had a reputation and history of its own. Considered a most favorable inn, William Thackeray lodged here in the 1820s and immortalized the tavern by mentioning it in his novel, *The Virginians*.

One cool evening while strolling around the inn yard, Thackeray saw an unusually attractive girl riding on a handsome charger. She was of Spanish origin. Thackeray and the lady became friendly but she was not inclined to supplement tales of his life in England and in India with the story of her life. She was, however, attracted by a large diamond ring which Thackeray wore. To impress the young lady he removed the ring from his finger and inscribed his name on one of the window panes (*Somerset American* 1979, 15 March).

In telling the tale, Thackeray added:

The massive north wall of the inn, made of mountain stone cut even, is painted black and on it appears the colossal figure of a white Conestoga horse, hence its name (*Somerset American* 1979, 15 March).

This section of the Glade Road came to be known as "White Horse Mountain." Early settlers handed down an interesting legend as to how both the inn and the mountain got its name. One version is that there was an Indian raid made on a number of travelers as they were driving their wagons over the mountain. It was during the time when the Pennsylvania frontier was aflame with Indian skirmishes by the Shawnee. The pioneers had stopped their wagons at a spring on the western side of the mountain. The wagons were burned and the pioneers scalped except for one young woman who was carried away by the Indians. The raid took place during a hard snowstorm. The settlers' horses were taken by the Indians but one white mare escaped into the woods. Subsequently, at varying times and places, the horse was seen by travelers on the mountain road. The legend of the horse gave the inn and this section of the Allegheny Mountains its name (*Somerset American* 1979, 15 March).

Another local narrative about the naming of White Horse Mountain concerns the original builder of the inn, Tobias Musser. He had underestimated the final cost of the building. It supposedly was in the original contract that if he failed to build the inn within the estimate that he would have to make up the difference in the form of a white horse. He failed and had to keep the contract with the payment of a white horse. The last remnants of the tavern, the stone wall mentioned by Thackeray, stood until 1914 when it was removed for a road location project (Fletcher 1971, 250).

Until the end of the eighteenth century, Pittsburgh remained set apart from the settled market cities of the Atlantic coast by the Allegheny mountain barrier. If the young western city was to prosper, a better means of transportation was needed. So began a series of turnpikes, roads built by individuals or companies, on which fees were charged. The term "turnpike" was derived from the hinged pole or pike which was placed as a barrier across the road at toll houses, and raised or turned aside after the required toll had been paid (Shank 1973, 4). Records show that the era of the turnpike in Somerset County dates back to 1806. At this time the Pennsylvania and Glade Roads were looked upon as being the most usable thoroughfares in the county (Fletcher 1971, 250). Yet for years to come, travelers who made the trip from Philadelphia to Pittsburgh in a "carriage and four," beheld with dread the cloud of dust that marked the slow approach of a train of wagons. Nothing excited the anger of the sturdy teamsters more than the sight of a carriage. It was the unmistakable mark of aristocracy (McMasters 1927, 1: 67-68). The social distinctions they had hoped to leave behind in England remained evident on the Pennsylvania Road.

Both the Pennsylvania Road and the Glade Road, to all intents and purposes, enjoyed an immense amount of traffic in the early years of the nineteenth century. A traveler on the Pennsylvania Road in 1817 had this observation:

Old America seems to be breaking up and moving westward. We are seldom out of sight of family groups. It is said that within the last year, 12,000 wagons, each drawn by four or six horses, and carrying great loads of merchandise, passed over the road. Add to these the numerous stages, filled to the utmost with passengers, and the innumerable travelers on horseback, on foot, and in light wagons, and you have before you an idea of the bustle and business along the route (Koontz 1906, 201).

PART TWO

Illustrious Citizens and Visitors

Somerset County was formed in 1795. Brunnerstown became the town of Somerset as well as the county seat. Isolated and remote, it remained a region largely removed from the main stream of Pennsylvania history. Nevertheless, its Sons of Thunder image tended to make it an exception to the rule that isolation results in obscurity. An extraordinary number of its citizens were to rise to positions of national prominence with names more important and better-known than their sequestered residence. Personalities of historical significance had a way of traveling the Old Forbes Military Road and recording their impressions. Many of these personal mementos furnish us with the truest accounts of what life west of the Alleghenies was like. From its founding, a chain of vibrant characters passed through the town and county and indelibly forged their names on local events and became intimately associated with local interests and people.

Echoes from the Iroquois

There is little evidence to prove Somerset County was the permanent settlement of any Indian tribes other than roving bands of Iroquois. Shawnee, Delaware and perhaps a tribe of the Algonquins may have lived within the borders of the county for an uncertain time, but for the most part there were not settlements of long duration. Mounds at Fort Hill and Fort Mclintock suggest the presence of Algonquins. But the region did become a treasured hunting ground for the Iroquois. Long after New England and Virginia Indian tribes had surrendered their jurisdiction, the Iroquois Nation continued to stand forth in bold colors on the canvas of Indian history. The Iroquois League of Nations was comprised of the Mohawk, Oneida, Onondaga, Cayuga and Seneca tribes, which lived in that order from east to west in central New York. Far from being the "savage brutes" early settlers found the native Indians to be, the Iroquois were highly intellectual beings who pondered deeply the eternal problems of men and nature. Like most tribes, they believed in a Supreme Deity, translated by the English to mean "Great Spirit," a pantheistic concept that varied from tribe to tribe and which was invoked with reverence. In a multilateral heaven, in the uppermost of these, the Great Spirit of the Iroquois dwelled (Terrell 1971; cf. Henry 1955, 27).

The founding of the Iroquois Confederacy has been described in a powerful and beautiful legend that the Iroquois held sacred. The founding of the league is lost in antiquity. Historians and anthropologists have made estimates that range from 1450 to 1660. Indian tradition favors the earlier date (Graymore 1972, 14). Because of their presence in southwestern Pennsylvania, Pennsylvania may have provided one of the first and greatest of the Native American myths to reach and become a part of the folklore of early Somerset settlers. Long one of the favorite characters of American folklore, Hiawatha was an American Indian who is best-known as the hero of Henry Wadsworth Longfellow's narrative poem, "The Song of Hiawatha." According to the poem, raised by his grandmother, Nokomis, Hiawatha was able to talk to the animals of the forest and surpassed all the young warriors in manly skills. He became a leader of the people, married the Indian maiden Minnehaha, and acted as a peacemaker among the warring tribes. The poem was inspired largely by Indian legends told by the student of Indian lore, Henry Rowe Schoolcroft. However, the hero of the poem is a composite of tribal legends based on the writings of Schoolcroft, which long attracted Longfellow.

Unlike the Hiawatha of the Longfellow poem, Hiawatha of the Iroquois was a chieftain of the Mohawks who lived in the late 1500s. He has no relationship to Longfellow's fanciful hero. Though bearing the name of the great Iroquoian reformer, the poem contains no single fact or diction relating to him, but is throughout full of Algonquin terms and legendary materials (Andrews 1962, 451). In the legend of the Iroquois is found the belief in the divine origin of the league assigned to two remarkable heroes, Deganawida and Hiawatha. The two leaders persuaded the five Nations to unite in friendship rather than continue with their destructive wars. Deganawida was a luminous figure; prophet, mystic, saint, and poet. Hiawatha was his first and foremost disciple (Henry 1955, 29). Following the wish and command of his mentor, Hiawatha advocated a new order of brotherhood among the tribes. The far-reaching ideals of the league were intended to be strong enough to embrace all mankind (Wallace 1945, 20).

It is difficult to separate the real Hiawatha of history from the many stories that later developed about him. In legend Hiawatha is a hero of miraculous birth becoming the incarnation of human progress with an orator's skill in moving people. His tender and lofty wisdom touched cords in the popular heart that continues until this day (30). Tradition credits him with introducing maize and fish oil to his people. He originated picture writing and the practice of medicine.

Hiawatha, the saintly wanderer, journeyed to the sunrise and then to the sunset; from as far south as the Pennsylvania mountains to the snowladen hemlocks of northern Ontario. His life was brought to an end as he walked slowly to the shore of Lake Onendya. Embarking in a canoe, he paddled westward. His grieving followers watched from the shore as his mystic craft disappeared into the setting sun. He was buried on the other side of the lake with his grave covered with hemlock bows (Henry 1955, 27). After his death his fame grew and he became a supernatural hero. The Iroquois league of Indian nations remained united and powerful until after the American Revolution.

Mountain Jack

While the territory known as Somerset County was still a part of Bedford, there appeared one of its most notorious and compelling personalities. He was known as Black Jack, Captain Jack, or Mountain Jack, the wild hunter. Though most of his activity took place in the Juniata Valley, both his person and legend brought him west of the Allegheny Mountains (Jones 1940, 136–137). This unusual backwoods character originally was from Philadelphia, the son of a Spaniard and a German housekeeper's daughter. As a boy, Mountain Jack only had minimal contact with his father whose visits to Philadelphia were infrequent and finally ceased altogether. During his rare visits, the adventurous Spanish sailor frequently told his wife an incredible tale of buried treasure. The story was passed on to Mountain Jack by his mother. Subsequently, Mountain Jack set out for the backwoods of southwestern Pennsylvania looking for the treasure he never found (Shoemaker and McVey 1916, 293). In 1773, the year before his death, he was known to be living in a cabin near a spring at the foot of the mountain that took his name, "Jack's Mountain."

The legend of Mountain Jack's fabled Spanish treasure begins in Madrid. Someone had devised a preposterous scheme to map an inland waterway between the Atlantic seaboard and New Spain. The route was to be up the Susquehanna River which somehow would join a utopian canal to Spanish possessions in the West. Disguised as traders and with Indian guides, the Spaniards, with bateaux and canoes, started up the river carrying sizable amounts of gold. Though the Spaniards and their Indian guides were on friendly terms, a night attack by another tribe left most of the party killed. Somehow, the gold had been hidden before the attack. Mountain Jack's father survived. He lay unconscious for some time, having been scalped and stripped of his clothing. Finally limping to the place where the canoe with the gold had been hidden he managed to steer himself to another island.

The canoe had been weakened by the heavy weight of the chest of gold. Faced with the choice of remaining on the island and building a new boat, or burying and abandoning the gold, he reasoned he must abandon the chest. Breaking the top before burying it, he removed some gold piece. After considerable effort he reached the main shore. Toward nightfall he sighted a lone Indian in a canoe. Of the Saponi tribe, the Indian took him prisoner, but gave him food and shelter. He was kept prisoner until spring, when he managed to escape. He returned to Philadelphia and eventually joined a ship returning to Spain (Shoemaker and McVey 1916, 293). The desire to find the gold that his father had buried was so strong that it took Mountain Jack into the woods of western Pennsylvania and kept him there.

Mountain Jack's savage eyes and dark complexion gave rise to many conjectures; one illustrated by the name Black Jack, due to the false belief that he was a half-breed Indian. His peculiar antics became part of a saga reaching all of Pennsylvania. For self-protection alone he became the relentless foe of the Indians (Ehrheart 1962, 2; Jones 1940, 135). "With an eye like that of an eagle and an aim that was unerring, he roamed the valleys and mountains like an uncaged tiger, the most formidable foe that ever crossed the Red Man's path" (Jones, 136). His ire was founded on the reality that his wife and children had been burned to death in their cabin home. Frequently, the bodies of Indians were found along the trail. Shooting from a distance, the Indians seldom heard his rifle. For this reason they called him "The Silent Rifle." He did seem to possess unearthly cunning and supernatural powers. It was claimed that he was almost as good as a moveable fort between Fort Bedford and Fort Pitt (Ehrheart 1962, 2).

The one great disappointment of Mountain Jack's life was that General Braddock refused his services in 1755. Mountain Jack claimed he could have saved the general and prevented the massacre at Great Meadows if he had acted as a scout of the party. Mountain Jack offered his services along with his band of hunters to General Braddock. Aware of his acumen on the frontier, George Crogan urged the British general to use him. Braddock viewed the recommendation as an insult. Many affirmed the belief that Mountain Jack could have changed the course of events if Braddock had taken the advice of Crogan. The British would "not have marched over the hill with drums beating and colors flying, in pride and pomp, as if enjoying a victory not yet won, but they would have the scouts out, the enemy and the position known" (Jones 1940, 137–138).

Mountain Jack was known to be a man of Herculean strength. After the Forbes Road had been built in the 1760s, Mountain Jack provided invaluable assistance in escorting soldiers and civilians to safety through the treacherous territory. When it was almost impossible to take a caravan from Fort Bedford to Fort Pitt without having the Indians kill a large number of the travelers, Mountain Jack frequently acted as a scout and helped to protect the wagon trains. He came into prominence when he organized a company of rangers who were dressed as Indians with hunting shirts, leather leggings and moccasins. They styled themselves "Captain Jack's Hunters." Governor Hamilton was quick to recognize the worth of the rangers and granted Mountain Jack a commission to keep the frontier Indians in check. His name became a part of the stories related not only by early settlers but by the Indians as well. Indians learned to keep their distance from him (Jones 1940, 137).

Popular belief held that he was buried near a spring at the foot of the mountain that bears his name. After his death, Mountain Jack's ghost became a traditional story among the early settlers. The legend held that every night at midnight his burly, swaying apparition would rise from the summit of the mountain and start down a moon-lit path to assuage his thirst at his favorite spring. Scores of reputable persons claimed to have experienced his appearance numerous times. He would reach out his right hand, as if he wanted to offer something. The legend lingers that Mountain Jack's ghost still clamors on the summit of his mountain at midnight (Shoemaker and McVey 1916, 293).[1]

The Night Vision of General John Forbes

Legends about the courageous spirit and exemplary character of General John Forbes were to linger long on the military road that made his name famous. The French intended to hold the strategic headwaters of the Ohio, where the Allegheny and Monongahela came together for the river as well as the territory west and north under the alleged discovery of the French explorer, Sieur De Rene Robert Cavalier Lasalle eighty years earlier. While the French had been first in the area, having settled there in 1603, they were never interested in or able to maintain settlements (Vogt 1976, 23).

Realizing matters were rapidly coming to a head, Britain sent General Braddock in 1755, and as we know, not until the arrival of General John Forbes in 1758, did French Fort Duquesne become Fort Pitt. This was followed by the Virginia historian Samuel Kurcheval in 1850 called "The War of 1763," by which the Treaty of Paris ceded French possessions to Britain after the fall of Quebec (Vogt 1976, 23).

Many references to General Forbes's illness can be noted but nothing is recorded about its nature or a specific diagnosis given. He was carried to Fort Duquesne in a hammock between two horses because he was unable to walk any distance. He was brought back to Philadelphia in a hammock supported by four of his Highlanders and accompanied by a piper. Frequent stops were made to give the general an opportunity to rest (Whisher 1978).

Upon reaching the summit of Ray's Hill, now Bedford, his aides found him quite exhausted by the time they arrived at a cabin occupied by a well-known hunter. He was carried into the cabin and placed upon a couch before a large fireplace. Legend quickly formed that he fell asleep and after some time rose from the couch and moved closer to the fireplace. In the glare of the fire arose the form of the love and passion that was to rule his secret life. Only the alertness of his men prevented him from falling into the fire. As he was lifted back to the couch, the general whispered that he had seen his Lady of Dunkirk, an apparition that came to him from the embers. He stretched his arm in an attempt to reach her and the vision disappeared (Whisher 1978).

One of Forbes's aides later enlisted for service in the Revolutionary War. When the war ended he returned to the cabin in the Alleghenies where he had spent the night with the general. Once settled, he enjoyed spending his evenings with friends and neighbors, recounting stories learned through his association with General Forbes. In nightly visits before the fireplace, with wine and candlelight, the retired officer disclosed that Forbes had spent the greater part of his life with the British military and little time in the company of women. As a young officer, Forbes had enjoyed the acquaintance of an older man and the hospitality of his home along the ocean in England. His revered friend had an eighteen-year-old daughter who fell deeply in love with Forbes. In his association with the family, Forbes never revealed or returned any feelings of affection for the girl. His devotion was to military life. Under the circumstances, the young woman declared an ultimatum; if he would not marry her she would disappear, never to be found.

Not insensitive to the situation, Forbes tried to reason with the girl that he was twice her age and could never make her happy. Her persistence was of no avail. After leaving the home of his friend, Forbes later was informed that the girl was missing. Upon receiving the news, he fell into a coma and remained so for almost a week. This supposedly was the beginning of the fainting seizures that were to plague him for the rest of his life. As the years went by and the distinguished general grew old, he spent many nights sitting alone before the fire hoping that perhaps, sometime, someway, he and the young woman would appear reunited (Whisher 1978). However, General Forbes's fondest dream was hidden from the real world. Oblivious to affairs of the heart but indebted to Forbes's significant contribution, the British would remain unaware. The heart of the Alleghenies preserved General John Forbes's "wonderful dream."

The Man Who Came to Turkeyfoot

George Washington was, and remains, Somerset County's most illustrious visitor. Of the numerous places where he supposedly slept, the environs of the county was one of them. His accommodations would not have been in gentlemanly fashion. They would not have included a well-appointed sleeping room, for inns and taverns did not yet exist. He would have taken his rest, most primitively sheltered, "under the stars."

On his first visit, Washington carried with him King George II's strict orders that the French were to be made to withdraw from the territory. The aristocratic Virginian was brought into Somerset County in the interests of the British to bring the French forces under control. He was accompanied by Christopher Gist as guide; John Davidson, an Indian interpreter; Jacob Van Braam, a French interpreter; and two frontiersmen. This was the first glimpse he had of Somerset County but government affairs would bring him back not less than eleven times. He would reach the headwaters of the Ohio and have his first glimpse of the strategic Gateway to the West. The youthful Washington on several occasions crossed the southwestern part of the county, exploring the valley where the Laurel Creek and Casselman Rivers converge with the Youghiogheny. The name "Turkeyfoot" was given to this part of the county (Doyle 1945, 38; cf. Cassady 1932, 9). His last visit in 1784 was again to the crossing where the three rivers converged (Doyle, 23).

The Arrival of Toscape Death

The man who recorded the most intimate and earliest account of Somerset County was the colorful and erratic Harmon Husband. Of Huguenot ancestry, Husband emigrated from North Carolina around 1770. While a resident of North Carolina he had acquired considerable property and had become a member of the state assembly. Fairly well-educated, he was believed to be closely related to Benjamin Franklin.[2] Husband became embroiled in the growing controversy between the colonists and England. The North Carolina state government, alarmed at Husband's treasonous attitude, proceeded to send armed forces against him and his associates. The result was rebellion; climaxed by the Battle of Alamance fought on May 16, 1771. Since Husband was a Quaker and his principles would not allow him to fight, he was forced by his convictions to leave. Evading his pursuers, Husband fled to the wilderness of Pennsylvania. Ironically, he took the name of "Toscape Death" and lived incognito as and with the Indians. There is a monument at Hillsboro, North Carolina, to twelve of his compatriots who were hanged by the British governor on June 19, 1771 (Doyle 1945, 46-47). Locating his cabin home within the eastern boundaries of what is now the town of Somerset, he later brought his wife and family into the western wilderness. This was believed to be the first family to settle in the area (Cassady 1932, 70).

With the outbreak of the Revolutionary War, pioneers of the region assembled under the command of Richard Brown to join General Washington's forces. Most families were evacuated to forts without benefit of supplies from their own lands. There are few detailed descriptions of the events that took place along the Forbes Military Road in Somerset County during the war, but it is known that the Indians used the road as a trail to eastern settlements. While settlers in the area lived in constant terror, there is no record of Indians having invaded this territory.

Following the Revolutionary War, the people embracing Somerset became involved in the nefarious Whiskey Insurrection and Harmon Husband with it. Hauling corn over the Alleghenies was an arduous task. Early settlers were little equipped for such heavy duty transportation. Converting corn to whiskey was a definite means to a controllable end. Eastern cities clamored for "a fine and robust liquor, made from the rich grain and inexhaustible supply of fresh mountain water." A heavy tax was levied on whiskey. Farmers rebelled. The tax led to more than just a revolt. It was an emotional issue. Secretary of the Treasury Alexander Hamilton, anxious to retire the national debt, believed that part of the money could be raised through an excise tax on distilled spirits. President George Washington agreed. Others disagreed, including Thomas Jefferson. He thought the excise "odious" and enacting a law would force the "authority of government in parts where resistance is most probable and coercion least practicable" (Ziukas 1994). Jefferson was thinking of southwestern Pennsylvania and his words proved it.

The penalty for nonpayment of the excise tax was standing trial in Philadelphia. The trip involved weeks of travel and lawyer's fees; both of which were potentially disastrous for the frontier farmer. With the arrival of federal troops to bring the rebellion under control, Husband as one of the outspoken leaders, was captured and taken to Philadelphia on charges that were later proven to be unfounded. After seven months imprisonment he was pardoned by President Washington. Starting for his home beyond the Alleghenies, his health broke and he died during the journey on June 19, 1795. Although politically erratic and a known religious fanatic, in saner moments Husband had a searching mind that left an indelible imprint on Somerset's early history. Husband had his finger on the throbbing pulse of colonial affairs of the day and through Benjamin Franklin, Jefferson and their contemporaries, he kept abreast of the great scientific discoveries of the age (Doyle 1945, 48). The Coffee Springs Farm, where he built his log cabin home, is still a prominent local landmark.

Cornplanter Closes a Ceremony

As the dark years of Pontiac's War passed into history, there remained one garrisoned British military fort in which the settlers could still take refuge—Fort Stony Creek. On March 31, 1762, Jacob Heckewelder, a Moravian missionary, accompanied by Charles Frederick Post arrived at the Stony Creek crossing. Heckewelder recorded that they found settlers living there who were independent of the military garrison that was maintained at the fort. Among the few who had established themselves along the Forbes Military Road was Casper Stotler. He had been attached to Bouquet's expedition and remained to brave the hardships of the early settlers. He lived in a cabin near the top of the Allegheny Mountains (Doyle 1945, 43).

An early account of an Iroquois episode within the county relates the tale of Rebecca Walters, who became Stotler's wife. She was captured as a child by Indians but later released. Some years after her marriage a delegation of twenty-five Indian chiefs with a military escort passed along the Forbes Military Road near where the Stotlers lived on their way to a conference with "White Fathers" in the east. It was evening when the delegation arrived. The officers requested permission to remain the night. As the Indians were building a fire near a spring Rebecca recognized several as belonging to the tribe that had held her captive. One of the old chiefs turned out to be Cornplanter, the great leader of the Senecas. The Seneca tribe was the most numerous, powerful and westernmost of the league members of the Iroquois. After visiting with Rebecca, the old chief asked permission to remain another day and night. Settlers came in large numbers to see the Indians who put on an exhibition of Seneca dances and customs. Cornplanter closed the ceremonies with the words:

38

These mountains were our hunting grounds and the arrowheads of our hunters are lying all around. I have been here in my youth. I chased the deer over yonder plain and drank the water from this beautiful spring (Baldwin 1964, 6).

Bibles West of the Alleghenies

Frederich Goeb, immigrating from Germany to Philadelphia, later settled in Somerset, sometime between 1806 and 1808. By 1810 he had established a log cabin print shop and was printing books in both English and German. He likewise published a weekly newspaper called the *Westliche Telegraph* (Western Telegraph) that was circulated throughout the county. He gave the town the distinction of producing in 1813 the first Bible printed west of the Alleghenies (Studer 1963). In this time period, printing a Bible in America was a tremendous task under the most favorable of conditions. Although Pittsburgh could claim the presence of a number of good printers, as of 1813, none attempted a printed edition of the Bible. By the time they did, Goeb had printed both a complete Bible and the New Testament at least five years earlier (Studer 1963, 2). In his prologue dated June 23, 1813, Goeb very modestly claimed only that his was the first German translation of the Bible published in Western Pennsylvania.

Goeb must have begun setting the type by 1810, or before; the tremendous volume in the translation of Martin Luther includes both Testaments, the Apocrypha and a table of feast of days. The printing of this Bible required setting close to five million pieces of type. Each page had to be set by hand and the type redistributed in the same way, for in that day no printer had either the type or space available to keep all the pages set up at once. The Goeb Bible is a ponderous volume more than a foot high and bound in leather over heavy oak boards nearly a quarter of an inch in thickness (Studer 1963, 4).

As of 1961, the American Antiquarian Society was able to discover only thirty-one copies. A year after publishing his Bible, Goeb published a smaller edition of the New Testament of which only twenty-nine copies are known to exist (Studer 1963, 6).

Of Goeb, the man, little is known. Were it not for the prologue to his edition of the Bible, his other publications, and a few scattered legal and public records, we would know almost nothing. His prologue, however, reflects the spirit of a deeply Christian man (Studer 1963, 6).

In the *Somerset Whig* of January 1, 1819, Frederich Goeb offers for rent his dwelling house in Somerset. This house is described as being large and well furnished, and on March 19, he announced a public auction at his house for the sale of his household effects with a "variety of English and German books." Soon afterward he moved to Shellsburg, Bedford County, where he was in the printing business by 1820 (Studer 1963, 6).

Other Visitors of Distinction

In the 1830s, two famous foreign travelers made their distinguished presence known in the Somerset area, but not in the most flattering terms. Their journals harshly recorded their deplorable journey over seven hazardous mountains and the exasperating weather conditions they endured while crossing the formidable Allegheny Mountains. Alexis de Tocqueville, representing the French government, traveled by coach from Philadelphia to Pittsburgh. He was journeying westward with his companion Gustave de Beaumont. Intent on gathering all the material they could on life in America, they talked to many citizens along the way, both famous and unknown.

On November 21, 1831, the young aristocrats were confronted with the rigors of a severe Somerset County winter. They were driven over what to them was the most gruesome section of the Pennsylvania Road, as it was then named. De Tocqueville, young and comparatively unknown at the time, would later distinguish himself for his perceptive and definitive masterpiece *Democracy in America*. Of all the books written about the United States and its institutions, perhaps none has been more significant. For more than 160 years it has helped Americans to understand their government, their character and the course of their history. Nearly as remarkable as the book itself is that its clear-sighted analysis and prophetic vision were the achievement of a French citizen. What different thoughts and feelings De Tocqueville had when he and his companion were experiencing a winter travel through Somerset County, unlike any they had known before. He records in his journal they were brutally assaulted by the frigid weather. Only after three exhausting days and nights, en route in bad carriages, over execrable roads, through an unending snowstorm, were they relieved of their ordeal (Jardon 1988, 164). Could anyone have rendered less painful their dismal situation, and wryly added a bit of humor to their despondency by informing them that they were in the land of the sturdy and stalwart "Frosty Sons of Thunder?"

Another celebrated European traveler who experienced the hazardous roads over the Alleghenies through Somerset County was Charles Dickens. Toward the middle of the nineteenth century he paid a visit to the United States, then returned to England with assembled notes that were to lend embellishment to writings and public addresses that mercilessly lampooned his American cousins. The rude and riotous frontier settlements received the full force of Dickens's vitriolic attacks. His portrayal of American life as it existed west of the Alleghenies was in the crude lines and black and white perspective of the cartoonist—a style of writing in which he was provokingly deft. Just as the cartoonist uses highlights to exaggerate and burlesque, so the famous novelist, with uncanny insight, selected outstanding characteristics upon which to focus his irrepressible wit and derision. His description of the frontier is not at all elegant, but, in some respects, it is surprisingly true. To Dickens, southwestern Pennsylvania was a "land of feverish swamps, slanderous newspapers and people exhibiting an unreasoning devotion to the 'American system of government'" (Pittsburgh Unit of the Federal Writer's Project 1937, forward). Whether it was due to the amazing progress of the people living west of the Allegheny Mountains or Dickens's own reevaluation of the environment, he reversed his attitude on his second visit.

The American poet, James Whitcomb Riley, had a more positive feeling toward both the town and county. His Hoosier dialect accents his deep regard for a land beyond his home. In an anthology of his verse is to be found, "'Mongst the Hills of Somerset" (see appendix A).

Jeremiah Black

Among the living legends of Somerset County, reference must be made to its most illustrious character, Jeremiah Sullivan Black. Jeremiah Black was a dynamic and colorful lawyer who had a great influence on American history in the nineteenth century. He became the first resident judge of Somerset County upon his appointment in 1842 at the age of thirty-one, and ultimately became one of the strong pillars of the Pennsylvania and American bench and bar (Brigance 1934, preface).

Somerset was a town of about 1,000 inhabitants at the time Jeremiah Black began practicing his profession. He seemed to epitomize a continuing saga of unusual and unique local personalities. In his journal, Ralph Waldo Emerson, in evaluating attorneys in Concord, Massachusetts, wrote, "A good many village attorneys we have, saucy village talents . . . but no great captains" (Baker 1996, 270). Somerset County's legal history would prove otherwise. There were numerous captains, among whom Jeremiah Black would rank a general. Under ordinary circumstances an able attorney in a small village might expect to find his way easier at the start through lack of competition or opposition from other lawyers. Somerset was a notable exception. From the very beginning of the settlement, the town was gifted with attorneys of unusual ability and wide experience. As for the people of the town in general, "the inhabitants were, unusually intelligent, many of them remarkably so. From this cold and rugged region came many of mark, so many that they have been collectively named, 'The Frosty Sons of Thunder'" (Clayton 1897, 29).

As a youth, Jeremiah Black had meager educational advantages despite the considerable prominence of his father, Henry Black. "I learned nothing," he said later, "except an intense dislike of confinement indoors." He once joined hands with other boys in seeking relief by searching for nails and pieces of iron among the ashes of a barn that had been struck by lightning and burned down. Firm in the belief that these were objects of proven and tested power in drawing lightning, they deposited them with great care under the schoolhouse and withdrew in serene confidence that the building would be demolished and their troubles ended. "I loved books but I hated school" became his own estimate of this period of his life (Clayton 1897, 11). Having no desire to partake in the ordinary amusements of youth, he never learned to swim, shoot, skate or play cards. His only recreation appeared to be reading and conversation. The latter he developed to a high art, not only as a means of expressing his own views, but also as a source of acquiring knowledge. A friend later wrote, "He plunders everyone he meets of all they know, and then it is his forever. . . . He talks all the time, but he wouldn't bore you if you made the trip with him from here to Pittsburgh by canal boat" (McClure 1905, 5).

Upon completing his academic studies, he turned his footsteps back to the family farm in Somerset and took his place behind the plow. It served him only as an accompaniment to the recitation of his favorite works by Dryden, Poe, Horace, Virgil and his beloved Shakespeare. In later years he added to his classical knowledge and became an avid reader of the Bible and fervent defender of the faith. He continued his education "behind the plow and the music of the crumbing soil. His lean frame was filling into the proportions of an unusually large man, tall, straight, supple, with the strength of a giant. His mind was a pace ahead of his body" (McClure 1905, 5). As a young man he introduced himself to the study of Shakespeare and became an avid scholar. "I never looked into Shakespeare until the second year of my study of law. Then I read and re-read all the plays until I became familiar with them. It was to me almost a new world" (Clayton 1897, 23). Eventually he knew the plays so perfectly that he no longer needed to read them.

At twenty-six, Black married Mary Forward, the eldest of Attorney Chauncey Forward's children. Black had served an apprenticeship in Chauncey Forward's office. Once involved, he became intensely interested in the study of law. Politics also attracted him strongly, but always and only in its relationship to law. "Law for him was the militant patriarch of justice. It spoke with the voice of the prophets" (McClure 1905, 283). He was later rewarded with honor and distinction. Jeremiah Black held several high offices: district judge and chief justice of Pennsylvania; attorney general and secretary of state of the United States.

Following the death of Andrew Jackson, Black delivered his eulogy at Bedford, July 28, 1845. He was now thirty-five. The address honored the life and character of Jackson and was received with acclamation. It brought Black prominently before the public. The closing pages contain sentences not only considered great in themselves, but in praising Jackson he unknowingly hit upon words which, to those who knew his character, described Black perfectly. "It is not once in a century that a man is born with the high moral courage which fits him to take the lead in a great reform" (Clayton 1897, 86). David Paul Brown, who had never heard of Black, remarked that "the best biography or memoir of General Jackson that was ever produced, was written by one Black from the backwoods of Pennsylvania, whom he, Brown had never seen, but would always admire" (24).

Meanwhile, a lasting friendship between Jeremiah Black and the future President James Buchanan developed. During Buchanan's presidency, Black was first appointed attorney general and then secretary of state. A native of Pennsylvania, Buchanan's presidency was severely marred by a nation divided over the problem of slavery. Throughout his administration the gap between the slave and the free states steadily widened and the president could find no way to deal with the critical question. Throughout the ordeal, Black remained the president's most devoted friend. In retirement, he continued to be his confidential advisor until Buchanan's death. Black befriended the president who was relentlessly under attack from critics in both the North and South for his compromise tactics. Buchanan fully appreciated Black, not only as a friend but as an astute politician whose advice he greatly respected. Buchanan intended to appoint Black a justice of the Supreme Court. Unfortunately, the nomination was delayed, and with the resignation of Southern senators the administration lost control of the Senate and Black's nomination was not acted upon. If he had been appointed to the Supreme Court he would have gone into history as one of the great jurists of the nation (Clayton 1897, 24). Through his startling eloquence the Supreme Court overthrew trial by military commissions in the North at the close of the Civil War. He also forced the Radical Congress of 1868 to repeal one of the Enforcement Acts of Reconstruction. "It is useless to deny it," said a justice of the Supreme. "Judge Black is the most magnificent orator at the American bar" (Brigance 1934, preface).

Famed as an eccentric, he reveled in his independence and his curiously egocentric life. Anathematizing the opinions of his political enemies, he had the rare ability to hold them as personal friends. Once denouncing certain of the justices of the Supreme Court for "having made a covenant with death," he continued to win decisions from that court (Brigance 1934, preface). At sixty, with his right arm crushed and rendered forever useless, he learned to write a beautiful script with his left. On the one hand Jeremiah Black was a gifted and fascinating conversationalist, but on the other he was noted for his most splenetic invectives. He reveled in controversies with such public figures as Stephen A. Douglas and Robert G. Ingersoll.

He was counsel for John C. Fremont: soldier, explorer, and

politician most famous as the Pathmarker of the West. Impulsive as a young man, with a checkered career both in military and civil life, Fremont lost the Republican nomination for the presidency to James Buchanan and later was involved in a scandal regarding the fraudulent sale of Memphis and El Paso railroad bonds in France. After a long investigation, Black finally obtained Fremont's release from a criminal conviction. Throughout the Buchanan presidency, Black worked in close association with Fremont, particularly on a plan for the abolition of slavery. Colorful, eloquent, arrogant and eccentric, Black was an "independent gladiator, hand in sword ready to champion minority causes."[3]

To the end of his life, Jeremiah Black remained a staunchly religious person. "But not of the churchly sort. His knee was too sturdy and his head too high to bend at any ritual or bow at a cleric's nod" (Koontz 1906, 409-10). To him there was no distinction between things religious and secular. . . . Theology was no more sacred than law" (Brigance 1934, preface).

Mr. President Comes to Somerset

Other than George Washington, Somerset's most distinguished visitor was President William McKinley. The Frosty Sons of Thunder had the distinction of having as a part of their heritage ties with two American presidents. In 1886, Abner McKinley, brother of the president, chose Somerset for his family's summer residence. The Victorian red brick mansion built on East Main Street came to be known as the "McKinley Place." It contained sixteen rooms and one of the first indoor bathrooms in the community. During his presidency, McKinley made two publicized visits to his brother's home in Somerset (*Somerset Herald* 1898, August 31). The national press referred to it as the "Summer White House." The first visit occurred in September 1897. It was the occasion of a week's holiday and pleasure. The *Somerset Herald* for August 31, 1898, reported that "the Chief Executive of the United States is a dignified, courteous gentleman, who grasps the hand of the humblest citizen with as much warmth as the gloved hand of royalty." The president and his wife held a public reception at McKinley Place attended by more than several hundred local residents.

The second visit of the president was to attend the spectacular wedding of Abner McKinley's daughter, Mabel. Front page news across

America reported in great detail the "two tons of wedding presents" received by the bride. The grand wedding was held at McKinley Place on September 12, 1900, near the bay window of the east drawing room under a bell covered with "thousands of white and pink roses." The wedding bell was as large as the "Independence Bell" and was seen by hundreds of people from outside. The president's niece was married to Dr. Hermanus Ludwig Baer, a local physician. Mabel McKinley Baer was to become a national celebrity as a result of her sensational music career. The president's affection for his niece was demonstrated by his gift in her honor of an organ to St. Paul's Presbyterian Church, which was located adjacent to McKinley Place (*Somerset Standard* 1900, September 13).

PART THREE

Somerset County's Versions of the American Antihero

The "Right Hand of David 'Robber' Lewis "

Of all of Pennsylvania's legendary heroes, none appears to be quite as daring and notorious as David "Robber" Lewis, the shrewd "Robin Hood of the Hills." Later to be overshadowed by the Nicely brothers in popular folklore, David "Robber" Lewis was a name to be reckoned with in the early nineteenth century. He sometimes occupied a mountain cave or caves near Somerset, hoping to escape capture by state authorities in the wilderness west of the Alleghenies. His infamous escapades were known as far away as New York and Vermont. He was the state and county's most notorious outlaw, counterfeiter and robber of his time.

The earliest record of the name David Lewis is associated with two other robbers in Bedford County in 1815 (Wallace 1962, 136-37). After robbing a man, Lewis's companions advocated killing him lest he become a witness against them. Lewis drew the line at murder, stating he "wanted no man's blood on his hands." He gave his victim a few dollars and permitted him to go on his way. Later that year he was arrested for four different offenses and charged with passing counterfeit money and bank notes. On February 17, 1816, he was tried, convicted and sentenced to six years imprisonment in the penitentiary at Philadelphia. He managed to break out of jail and escape. Later recaptured, he was imprisoned but pardoned by Governor Findley (Hall 1890, 250). Powerful political influences were believed to have been brought on the governor to bring about the pardon, which may have contributed to his defeat for reelection in the fall of 1820. As a result of a gunshot wound, Lewis died in the Bellefonte County jail in

1820. After his death there appeared a pamphlet entitled "The Confession of David Lewis," by James Duncan, Lewis's attorney at the time of his trial for desertion from the army. The confession contained the salient facts of his life and his bold but short career. From this emerged the legend of the Right Hand of "Robber" Lewis (258).

David Lewis was born on March 20, 1790, near Carlisle, Pennsylvania, of poor but respectable parents. He was one of a large number of children. His father died when David was less than ten years old. For the next seven years he remained with his mother and assisted in rearing the other children. He worked at several occupations until enlisting in the army. Supposedly punished by an army sergeant for a minor offense, he deserted, later to reenlist under an assumed name. Nevertheless he was soon discovered and recognized as a deserter and sentenced to death. Army discipline was known to be extremely rigid just prior to the War of 1812. After serving a week of his sentence, Lewis managed to escape. This was the beginning of his long and varied career of robbery and lawlessness.

Lewis's activities as an outlaw found him victimizing country banks whose notes were easy to counterfeit. Discovering that the most expert counterfeiters operated in Vermont, he journeyed there and engaged in making enormous quantities of spurious bank notes, which he later passed in New York state. Again captured and committed to a jail in Troy, he managed another escape with the help of the jail keeper's daughter who fled with him and whom he later married.

With his new bride he lived briefly in Albany and from there went to New York City, where he fraternized with the most notorious racketeers. While in New York City, he learned that Mrs. John Jacob Astor was to attend a well-publicized auction sale. The day of the auction Mrs. Astor made purchases of rare lace and jewelry that she placed in a large net handbag. While she was engaged in conversation, Lewis snatched her handbag and made his escape. He headed for Princeton, making his headquarters in New Brunswick, New Jersey, where he lived with his wife. She supposedly was kept in absolute ignorance of his activities. A daughter was born to them during this time.

At Princeton, Lewis made his inauspicious presence felt at the university where he is said to have found "empty heads and full purses." He was believed to have fleeced many of the Princeton students of their allowances as they were singing their way "Back to Nassau Hall."

Leaving his wife and child in New Brunswick, his next exploit was in Philadelphia, where he became the leader of a band attempting to kidnap the eminent financier, Stephen Girard. Taking Girard out of the city and into the country, the prisoner was confined until forced to purchase his freedom. An attempt was made to dig a tunnel from Philadelphia's Dock Street sewer to Girard's banking house where bank vaults could be reached, but a dangerous illness of Lewis's daughter interrupted the plan. The gang drifted apart and the scheme was abandoned.

David Lewis was reputedly a man of unusual physical strength. Legend claims he was straight and tall with sandy hair, long arms and thin hands. He was aware that he had the ability to attract others, particularly those who accompanied him on his infamous journeys through Pennsylvania, who gladly aided him in his numerous escapades and escapes. His performances became proverbial. Many a signal was raised from an upper story window denoting that the way was clear for him to pass, or that food would be brought to one of his many mountain cave hiding places. One such hiding place was believed to have been in Somerset County, near Stoystown (Hall 1890, 258), where he manufactured a large supply of counterfeit bank notes later circulated through Bedford and Somerset Counties. Here he learned that his wife had died while giving birth to their second child. He continued with his operations. Counterfeiters were legion in the early part of the nineteenth century, so much so that a book description of counterfeits became the necessary appendage of a merchant's store.

A personal adventure with Lewis in the Allegheny Mountains was reported by a man known only as Black, from Cumberland, Maryland. Black had crossed the mountains on horseback to Brownsville where he collected a large sum of money. While in Brownsville, he won another horse in a gambling race. The following day he started home with two horses and a sizable money purse. A man appeared in a lonely ravine and jumped on the back of the accompanying horse. He rode alongside Black and began to barter for the horse. Black informed the intruder that the horse was not for sale. As they rode on, eventually dismounting for something to eat and perhaps a nip of peach brandy, they became more intimate. The stranger asked Black if he had ever seen Lewis the "Robber." Black claimed he had not. "Well," said the stranger, "here is Lewis, I am the man." Lewis informed Black that he had witnessed the race in Brownsville and knew that Black was in possession of a large sum of money. Lewis informed Black that he had intended to rob him, but because of his gentlemanly characteristics had decided to let him go.

Another time, a large party in search of Lewis met a well-dressed stranger on horseback and asked if he had seen or heard anything of Lewis. He replied that he had not and joined in the pursuit. Sometime later one of the members of the party was to receive a letter stating that he had been riding with Lewis. The writer of the letter was anxious to learn if he, and the members of the party, had found the stranger agreeable.

One of the most often told tales of the Lewis cycle is included in the folklore of nearly every venerated outlaw. Asking for overnight lodging in the obscure home of a country widow, Lewis learned that the widow was in deep trouble because the mortgage of her house was due and the local constable was to arrive the next morning to foreclose on the property. Lewis, living up to his long-standing reputation, gave the woman the necessary amount and insisted that she receive a receipt from the constable. When Lewis left the next morning, the constable arrived, the necessary business was transacted and the constable went away with the payment but not the property. On top of the mountain, the constable was met by "Robber" Lewis who presented his pistol and took the money that had been loaned to the widow, as well as forty dollars belonging to the constable. Lewis later boasted that the short loan of money to the woman was the best investment he had ever made. Lewis became a legend because of the strong hold he had on the country people. Though they admired his boldness and poise, his misdeeds may be traced to the court records of Somerset, Bedford, Mifflin and Center Counties.

Often captured, Lewis was never long confined. By one trick or another he always managed to escape. In June 1820, near Bellefonte, Lewis and a companion waylaid and robbed a wagon transporting store goods. Lewis, pursued by a posse of well-armed and resolute men, was discovered while shooting mark with pistols. The posse demanded that he and his companion surrender. They refused. Lewis's companion was killed in the melee that followed and Lewis was shot in the right arm near his elbow. Taken prisoner and jailed in Bellefonte, a local physician informed him that his wound had developed gangrene and that his only chance to stay alive was to have his arm amputated. This he refused to do. Life without his good arm had no appeal. He died on July 30, 1820, at thirty years of age, and was buried in the jail cemetery.[1] Tradition holds that his only daughter became a resident of Harrisburg where she lived respectably the remainder of her life (Hall 1890, 258).

The spirit of David Lewis lived on in the many legends that developed about him along the Pennsylvania Road. The next scene to open upon his posthumous ventures is portrayed in the White Horse Tavern in old Somerset County, along the Bedford Pike, now Route 31.

Early one morning in the fall of 1820, a mysterious young horseman appeared at the tavern, regal in his presence and mounted on a superb black horse. He made his presence known just as the innkeeper's daughter, Dowsabel Casselman, was about to draw water from the well. Tipping the brim of his hat ever so lightly, he politely asked if he might have a drink of water. The shy and flustered Dowsabel took a gourd, filled it with water, and offered it to him. The innkeeper's daughter was known to be a mountain beauty that the young stranger was quick to recognize. Their conversation was pleasant but brief, and the mysterious stranger continued his journey toward Somerset. Hardly had he departed when he was replaced by an old man who came and stood with Dowsabel beside the well. He also asked for a drink of water. Dowsabel, lost in dreams of her departed knight, shrugged the old man off as she left him to get his own water. His cryptic and prophetic response went unheeded by the young girl, as he scornfully replied, "When that stranger is through with you, you will lead an ape in hell. We will meet again."

Several weeks passed as Dowsabel continued to pine for the young stranger, who returned as she fondly had hoped he would. His further conversations with the impressionable and smitten Dowsabel revealed that his true name was David Perverey. He was known in the mountains as "Young Lewis," for his only ambition was to follow in the footsteps and make his every action characteristic of the renowned David Lewis. Knowing the overburdened young girl was bored with her existence and obviously enamored with him, he offered her what he knew would be an enticing proposition that she could not refuse.

"I will take you away with me," he said, "but first you must prove your fitness to be with me."

She listened intently as he told her that in order to win his love, she must secure for him that which he most wanted, the right hand of David Lewis. It was believed to possess miraculous charm, but had to be cut from the corpse which lay in the Bellefonte jail yard. A well-

51

founded legend already had developed along the Pennsylvania Road that anyone possessing the right hand of David Lewis could exercise a spell over those with whom he came in contact. Young Lewis not only wanted to exercise the spell; he already was under it. He continued by saying that in order to accomplish the task, Dowsabel must abscond with her father's carriage, secretly drive to Bellefonte, register in the Brenner Hotel and wait for the bills that would be posted announcing the reward for her capture as a runaway. Once taken into custody and housed in the Bellefonte jail, she would be in safekeeping until her father would come to claim her. In the meantime, she must exhume the body of David Lewis, break the right hand from the wrist, and climb to freedom over a twenty foot wall.

Young Lewis's demands were quite a feat for any criminal, let alone the demure and inexperienced Dowsabel. Yet the lovesick girl was determined to follow through with her lover's outlandish instructions. Hardly had she settled in the Brenner Hotel when she was recognized and marched off to the Bellefonte jail, awaiting her father's willing ransom. The remainder of the incredible request was carried out with almost miraculous precision. Escaping at night from her cell, severing the bars with a saw that Young Lewis had given her, she cleverly broke the rusty lock and calmly walked into the jail yard. Alternately using a pick and shovel standing against a stone wall, Dowsbel labored at opening the grave of David Lewis in the half frozen snow. Finally, she managed to get hold of the crumbly right arm, deftly twisting off the hand at the wrist. Then, in the dead of night, instead of scaling the impossible jail house wall, she boldly walked through the rooms of the jail house and out into the street where Young Lewis awaited her in a covered carriage.

Some days later, a hooded carriage drew up in front of the old stone tavern in Millerstown. A young girl descended, walked into the tavern and asked for accommodations. No other guests were in the tavern at the time. She was led into the kitchen, the only lighted room. Sitting close to the stove, Dowsabel was startled when the old man who had approached her at the well of the White Horse Tavern entered the room. There was no chance of escape. Her screams for assistance served Young Lewis, her black knight of the road, who believed that his possession of the right hand of David Lewis was about to become his lucky talisman. He laid a long, strong whip over the horse's flanks and fled into the night, leaving Dowsabel the victim of her fate.

Gagged by the old man, bewildered and dazed, Dowsabel was held prisoner in the kitchen of the tavern. Since he held her prisoner, would he not receive the reward? Or at least part of it? Yet other thoughts passed through the mind of the old codger and twisted the key of fate. He quickly removed a gypsy dagger from a long sheath, cut the ropes which bound Dowsabel's wrists and ankles, and bade her leave the tavern. When she had gone the old man turned and looked upon the face of a tall clock that stood in the corner of the kitchen, which had painted on its face the strange Biscayan proverb, "Every hour wounds. The last one kills." The clock struck three (Shoemaker 1928, 1:4).

Early the next morning the innkeeper and his wife came into the kitchen to find no trace of the young girl or the old man (Shoemaker 1928, 1:4). Yet later that night as they lit an evening fire for traveling guests, they related the peculiar happenings that had taken place in the tavern. It would become a sequel to the tale of "Lewis the Robber," and become known as the "Right Hand of David 'Robber' Lewis" (Doncaster 1985, 26:3). It remained a favorite legend along the Pennsylvania Road until 1889 when, on a February night, two men from Ligonier crossed the Laurel Mountain on their fateful journey to the home of Herman Umberger. The Lewis legend was lost in public memory to give way to the more spectacular story derived from the lives of Joseph and David Nicely.

The Legend of the Nicely Brothers

The Narrative of a Crime

Several days after the United States celebrated the one hundredth anniversary of the inauguration of George Washington, one of Somerset County's most prominent farmers was robbed in his home and murdered in the presence of his wife. Three months later, concurrent with the Johnstown flood, Joseph and David Nicely, from nearby Ligonier, were convicted of the murder. Their trial in the Somerset County Courthouse became a sensation and a situation that aroused more public interest than any trial previously held or relating to any other person previously known in the county. Two years later, after an incredible series of circumstances, Joseph and David Nicely were hanged in the Somerset County jail. Their story ended in the presence of eight hundred mourners, most of whom continued to proclaim the innocence of the Nicely brothers. Their remains from the family farm are located in the Grandview Cemetery in Ligonier, Pennsylvania.

Somerset County farmers were frugal men—God fearing and law abiding. Next to their Bibles they most revered the *Hagerstown Almanac*. Rarely was timber cut without consulting its calendar. Pages became soiled and worn that dealt with varying phases of the moon. Word had been passed down from generation to generation that trees cut in February, when the moon was in its fourth quarter, made the best lumber for building (*Greensburg Morning Review* 1974, 7 July). Structures were certain to remain straight and firm. A combination of frugality, a tinge of the New England Protestant ethic, and a bent toward the superstitious formed the background for Somerset County's Pennsylvania Dutch. The Herman Umberger family was characteristic of settlers in the area.

Near Jennerstown, some eleven miles north of Somerset, on Wednesday evening, February 27, 1889, the crime took place in the parlor of the Umberger home. The morning after, Somerset County residents were startled by a report that a widely known farmer had been murdered in the presence of his family. Herman Umberger, a bearded, taciturn man in his early 70s, was one of the county's most prosperous yet illusive farmers. His 200 acre farm along the Johnstown Pike, some two miles off the Pennsylvania Road, was a well-known landmark. The two-story frame farmhouse was located on the west side of the road at the foot of a small hill. A large cattle barn faced the house.

Well-circulated rumor held that Herman Umberger was a farmer of substantial means, but equally miserly peculiarities. Skeptical of banks, he kept a sizeable sum of his country fortune, considerable for the times, hidden in two well-worn pocketbooks in a bureau in the downstairs bedroom. The bulging wallets had been viewed on occasion, in direct line from the parlor where the prosperous old gentleman engaged in conversations concerning financial matters. The wallets and their contents were privately as well as openly appraised by inquisitive relatives and curious neighbors. Umberger added to his substantial means by lending money on firmly secured notes. A stern-faced man, abrupt and exacting, he demanded prompt payment from his debtors. Snidely respected for his business acumen by acrimonious money changers, yet feared as a creditor, the name Herman Umberger was recognizable throughout the county, connoting Calvinistic thrift to some, niggardliness to others.

The evening of February 27 was a dismal, "dead of winter" night. Snow had partly melted. Only an occasional drift remained. Roads were soft with mud and slush. Wooded areas along the mountain ravines remained carpeted with snow. Following the evening meal, as the dark night fell ominously on the Umberger home, the small family gathered around a wood stove in the rural Victorian parlor. Other than Herman Umberger, present in the home that evening were his third wife,[2] Nancy, to whom he had been married for thirty years; Mrs. Umberger's granddaughter, ten-year-old Nannie Horner; and the hired girl, Ella Stern. Nannie's eighteen-year-old brother, George, had been helping with the work about the farm during the recent illness of Umberger. Earlier in the evening, he had gone to the grocery store of Wesley Griffith at nearby Berkley's Crossroads to be with friends.

Herman Umberger became ill on New Year's Day and was still confined to his home. Recovering slowly, he spent the long February evenings in an armchair near the wood stove. With the month nearly over, no trees had been cut on his property, which was cause for concern according to the almanac. The stillness of the dreary evening was interrupted by the sharp staccato sound of sleet upon the windows and the crackling noises of the wood fire. The family was by nature silent and introspective, each absorbed in his own thoughts and solitary activity.

Shortly after 7:00 P.M. a knocking was heard on the front door. Despite the cheerless evening or the abruptness of the knocking, no one appeared dismayed or overly concerned. Ella Stern was directed to answer. When she opened the door, the curtain rose on the curious and enigmatic Umberger-Nicely drama that might vary in interpretation but would never lose its rustic mystique. Out of the night's bleakness emerged two sinister figures, oddly disguised, who were fearlessly led by the young woman into the sitting room. Local custom and conventional hospitality called for hosts to be cordial to strangers. Chairs were provided and placed near the stove. Despite a parsimonious reputation, Herman Umberger was a conforming man. Often disliked for the severity of his nature, propriety led him to invite the men to take chairs and warm themselves by the stove.

Viewing the evening in perspective, one wonders why Herman

Umberger, being otherwise cautious and normally suspicious of wayfarers, had been so unsuspecting of what amounted to a forced entrance into his home. The disguised appearance of both men was strangely peculiar, verging on the bizarre. For a man of Herman Umberger's temperament and cultural proclivities, the curious men were unsuited for parlor conversation in the Umberger home or for country hospitality.

The night visitors were heavily bundled in oversized overcoats. One of the men was considerably taller than the other. The taller man had on a pair of brown overalls with yellow stripes and had two red and white dotted handkerchiefs tied about his face exposing only his eyes. He had on leather boots (Werner 1890, 23). Little of his features could be seen. The smaller man explained that his companion had been thrown from a buggy and that his face had been injured, resulting in the need for the handkerchiefs. The little man had on dark clothing and wore gum boots and a brown derby hat. There was a hole in the brim of the hat (Werner, 24). The little man did all the talking.

At this point the unusual intruders should have aroused some suspicion. The odd masquerade of the tall man was matched in idiosyncratic attire by a gray wig and false beard worn by the smaller man. The stage was set complete with costumes and characters.

The smaller man claimed they were law officials from Bedford. They were carrying warrants that permitted them to recover a quantity of jewelry that had been lost by a peddler named Moxam. He informed the Umbergers that they already had searched the houses of neighboring Gillian Friedline and Franklin Heiple. Further, they had been instructed to search every house between Jennerstown and Johnstown. A paper purporting to be a search warrant was read.

After a half-hour conversation on matters dealing with the weather and spring planting, Herman Umberger rose from his chair and joined in the supposedly warranted search. Ella Stern went into the kitchen and returned with a lighted candle that she gave to Herman Umberger. While she remained with the taller man in the sitting room, the tour of the downstairs began, including the smaller man, Herman and Nancy Umberger, and Nannie Horner. The parlor, the kitchen and finally the downstairs bedroom were searched. As the night's activities were quickly to change into local legend, the masked men gained the dubious names of the "Tall Man" and the "Small Man."

Up to this point, neither Herman Umberger nor his wife expressed any form of outward dismay. But with the curious thoroughness of the oddly dressed man, their suspicions turned gravely apprehensive. They made an attempt to distract the Small Man from their bedroom where Herman Umberger's pocketbooks were kept in the upper drawer of the largest of two bureaus. The pocketbooks, well-recognized by anyone having had business dealings with Herman Umberger, were generally appraised to contain a sizable sum of money (Werner 1890, 4-5).

The Small Man's search of the sitting room and kitchen was abrupt and hurried. The Umbergers were quick to perceive that when they entered the bedroom the probing became slower and more thorough. He insisted on examining, drawer by drawer, the two bedroom chests. One was searched and nothing found. When Nancy Umberger opened the top drawer of the second bureau, the Small Man quickly caught sight of the pocketbooks.

Upon returning to the parlor, the Umbergers believed the search was over. But the Small Man abruptly announced he wanted to go back to the bedroom. He had forgotten to look under the bed. By this time Nancy Umberger's womanly intuition and Pennsylvania Dutch upbringing made her starkly aware of the absurdity of the situation. Growing more and more impatient, particularly at the moment when they returned to the bedroom, the Small Man commanded her to empty the top drawer of the chest. Nancy Umberger refused. In caustic tones she ordered the intruder to complete his search and leave as soon as possible. It was evident that he had seen the pocketbooks. Sensing this, with the Small Man's back to him, Herman Umberger removed the pocketbooks from the drawer and placed them in his vest pocket.

Back in the parlor again, the Small Man suddenly turned toward Herman Umberger and demanded the pocketbooks. In the split seconds that followed, the Small Man whipped out a revolver. The ensuing melee forced the pocketbooks from Herman Umberger's vest. They fell to the floor. In attempting to retrieve the pocketbooks, Nancy Umberger unknowingly tramped on a lamp chimney that the Small Man apparently had used to look for the pocketbooks. Herman Umberger was forced to a corner of the room. Four or five shots resounded from the revolver of the Small Man. Two of the bullets entered Umberger's body, one in the shoulder and the other penetrating his heart. Reeling under the impact of the bullets, he staggered into the kitchen. All the while, the Tall Man remained inconspicuously in the background, the entire search and ultimate murder of Herman Umberger being managed by the Small Man (Koontz 1906, II: 201).

Rural homes of the era had warning bells that served as a dinner bell during the day and an alarm at night. The sound of a night bell signaled neighbors to a fire or an emergency. The Umbergers' bell pull was just inside the kitchen. As the burglars made their escape into the night, a bewildered Nancy Umberger stumbled to reach and ring the bell. Her severely wounded husband followed, and seconds later fell and died at her feet.

Ella Stern and Nannie Horner, frightened beyond reason, ran out of the house. Their screams soon brought a number of mystified neighbors to the farmhouse. By the time they arrived, the murderers had distanced themselves from the scene with Herman Umberger's pocketbooks in their possession. Making their way up the western slope of the Laurel Ridge, the masqueraders had escaped into the darkness with the sum total of Herman Umberger's worth. They left behind no clues other than the sound of their voices and footprints in the mountain snow.

Early the next morning, several hundred persons quickly gathered near the Umberger residence. According to Mrs. Umberger an estimated $16,000 to $20,000 was believed to have been stolen including some gold pieces (Werner 1890, 7). As friends and relatives assembled, Perry Umberger, brother of Herman, in consultation with Mrs. Umberger, determined to offer a reward of $2,000 for the return of the money and $8500 for the arrest and conviction of the murderers. The decision also was made to procure the services of the Gilkinson Detective Bureau of Pittsburgh.

News of the murder and robbery spread rapidly. The excitement throughout the county for the next six or eight weeks was without precedent. Public indignation reached a fever pitch. Traditionally peaceful and law-abiding citizens called for the immediate capture and lynching of the murderers.[3] Because Somerset County lacks any history of great significance, other than the part the Forbes Military Road played in the French and Indian War, the Nicely Brothers' trial and conviction became the county's most enduring history turned legend (cf. Koontz 1906). The tragedy, with all its ramifications, was an event without parallel in the history of Somerset County, Pennsylvania. D. A. Gilkinson, superintendent of the Pittsburgh Detective Bureau, felt the case of such importance that he departed the following Monday morning to head a search for the murderers personally. In the meantime, Somerset officials already were pursuing what few leads they could find. Constable John O. Rauch of Jennerstown had gone to Mount Pleasant for the purpose of arresting two suspects, but the initial investigation was shortened when it became evident that the Mount Pleasant men were not guilty (Werner 1890, 7).

Three men from nearby Jennerstown returned to the Umberger home the following Thursday evening and reported that they had followed tracks in the snow of the mysterious Tall Man and Small Man over the Laurel Ridge. Tracks had been traced through the fields above the Umberger farm leading down the western slope of the Laurel Ridge to a place known as Burnt Cabin, within three miles of the village of Laughlinstown. Here was the residence of a notorious young outlaw named Collins Hamilton, who made his home with two elderly woman relatives, keepers of a tollgate along the Pennsylvania Road now Route 30, also called the Lincoln Highway. Because of previous misdemeanors (Werner 1890, 8), suspicion now rested heavily with Collins Hamilton. He was arrested that evening and committed to the jail in Somerset.

A further lead was to prove far more significant. Somerset County authorities claimed to be in possession of facts that pointed toward two men living in a rural section of the nearby village of Ligonier, Westmoreland County. Since his initial search in Mount Pleasant proved to be in vain, as did the arrest of Collins Hamilton, Constable Rauch refocused his investigation in Ligonier on the western side of the Laurel Mountain. A number of people living in the neighborhood intimated that two residents of the Ligonier Valley had been suspected of committing numerous local robberies. This information, together with circumstantial evidence gathered from Herman Umberger's murder, lowered an ominous cloud on David and Joseph Nicely. The Nicely brothers lived some three miles south of Ligonier on farms adjacent to that of their better-known and highly respected father, Anthony A. Nicely (Werner, 8).

In the spring of 1889, neither Johnstown nor Somerset could match Ligonier in historical significance. Situated on the Loyalhanna River (meaning "middle stream") and named by the Delaware Indians, the town was halfway between the Juniata at Bedford and the headwaters of the Ohio in Pittsburgh. The Pennsylvania Road went directly through it. Its historical prominence came into being when in 1758, General John Forbes arrived with his British army. A string of forts and supply depots had been built from Carlisle to Pittsburgh. Ligonier was the last in the series and was named in honor of Lord John Ligonier, then commander in chief of all British armies. The fort was an active military post for nearly two decades, serving as a communication point and supply center for Fort Pitt and the Ohio Valley.

Through the historic valley passed thousands of stagecoach travelers in the early nineteenth century along with westbound immigrants and settlers. Eventually peace settled over the region and the Ligonier Valley entered a long and productive life. Its good soil supported many pioneer farms and it enjoyed the protection of two natural boundaries—the Laurel Mountain on the east, and the Chestnut Ridge on the West. The area was most attractive to frontier families, including the immediate ancestors of Anthony A. Nicely. Indeed, Nicely was a respected name in the Ligonier Valley and a part of local legend long before intimations of guilt for murder fell upon Joseph and David Nicely.

In the far reaches of Ligonier's provincial history, sometime during the summer of 1790, while picking blackberries with his brothers and sisters, five-year-old Jacob Nicely was captured by a band of Indians. He was a son of Adam Nicely. The family lived on the Four Mile Run about two miles from its junction with the Loyalhanna River. With several companions, Adam Nicely, in pursuit of the captors of his son, followed as far as the Kiskiminetas River where they lost the trail. No trace of the captive child was found.

Legend holds that years later, a man who traded with the Senecas in Warren County recognized Jacob and brought the information to Jacob's mother, who was then in her seventies. A brother traveled to the Seneca reservation and found Jacob. The brothers recognized each other and Jacob related that he had been adopted by the Indians, grown to manhood with them and acquired an Indian family and considerable possessions. Some time prior to 1828, Jacob made a return journey in an effort to locate his relatives. He had a brief visit with them and promised to return again to visit his aged mother. The promise was never fulfilled (Sipe 1932, 624-25).

Anthony A. Nicely was a later descendent of the Adam Nicely family. Devoid of Herman Umberger's pecuniary proclivities, he was by nature a more compassionate and harmonious man. Anthony Nicely was equally well known, but respected in a different way from his Somerset counterpart. He was recognized as a straightforward, white-haired old gentleman with a kind and intelligent face. Known throughout Westmoreland County, he was highly esteemed by neighbors and friends. His name was placed among those of the more prosperous farmers. He was generous with his family, and both David and Joseph received sections of his farm. Despite the unsavory reputations of his sons, the family generally was respected in the community and enjoyed a congenial family life.

Relatively happy and enjoying comfortable circumstances. Anthony Nicely and his wife Elizabeth had several children who lived in close proximity to the family farm. Both Joseph and David were married with several children. Each lived a short distance from the other. At the time of Herman Umberger's murder, David was twenty-five and Joseph was forty. The brothers had at one time shared a partnership in a small hotel in Ligonier.

When news of the murder of Herman Umberger reached Ligonier, there was mounting suspicion that the brothers were guilty of the crime because of their history of misdeeds. On Monday, March 4, Officer Rauch and his party from Jennerstown hired a carriage and proceeded to the residences of the Nicely brothers and promptly arrested them. Clothing identified as that worn by the Tall Man and the Small Man on the night of the murder was discovered in their respective homes. At Joseph Nicely's home officials located a pair of yellow striped trousers worn by the Tall Man on the night of the murder. Also discovered was a red handkerchief with white spots, an overcoat and a pair of boots such as worn by the Tall Man. A search of David's house resulted in locating a pocketbook believed to be that of Herman Umberger. Discovered also was a low derby hat with a hole in the brim and a dark colored suit of clothing, later identified by Nancy Horner and Ella Stern (Werner 1890, 30–31). There also were several letters uncovered making reference to "green goods." When Joseph Nicely was arrested he was wearing a pair of gum boots, which supposedly corresponded to tracks made in the snow over the Laurel Ridge. A 32-caliber revolver believed to be identical to the gun used in the murder and a number of cartridges, the same size as those taken from the body of Herman Umberger, were found at Joseph Nicely's house.[4] Upon further investigation Gillian Friedline and Mrs. Joseph Walter identified the brothers and claimed to have seen them cross the

Laurel Ridge the day of the murder. Lewis W. Vannear also made a positive identification.

Authorities believed they had collected enough evidence not only to arrest the brothers but to charge them with murder. Joseph and David Nicely were arraigned and kept the night in the National Hotel in Ligonier. The following morning they were taken to Jennerstown where a hearing was held before Justice Henry Rauch. Both men were identified by Nancy Umberger, whose unequivocal belief was that the brothers were the men who murdered her husband (Werner, 9). Ella Stern also was certain in her identification. When Joseph Nicely spoke, she claimed, positively, to recognize his voice. When David Nicely removed a red handkerchief covered with round white dots from his pocket, Ella Stern exclaimed that he held the same handkerchief she had seen on the night of the murder. She was quite definite in her opinion that the two brothers were the murderers. Joseph and David Nicely were then placed in the Somerset jail and held for court.

In the days and weeks that followed their initial arrest, Somerset and the Nicelys became a topic of conversation that would forever link the town and the brothers. Spectators, many not counted among the local residents, began to crowd about the jail daily, morbidly fascinated by newspaper accounts of the diabolical murder believed to have been committed by the brothers. The arrest and commitment of David and Joseph Nicely created a sensation not only in the town but throughout the state. The course of their lives became cause for a variety of speculative opinions.

Joseph Nicely would have been recognized and acclaimed a handsome man. He was gifted with striking features—dark piercing eyes and a quixotic smile that played around the corners of his mouth. A heavy moustache ornamented his upper lip. He was neat in appearance and wore clothes that were well-fitting. He sang with a resounding tenor voice. Although small of stature, he was athletically inclined and at the time of his arrest showed remarkable strength.

David, on the other hand, was more taciturn and subdued. Thin and tall, he "walked as erect as a Sioux chief." Since confined to the Somerset jail he rarely talked without consulting his brother. The younger and more retiring of the two, he appeared to be entirely under the influence of Joseph and depended upon him to do the talking and to make decisions. Anytime the brothers appeared together, Joseph's strong shadow shrouded the laconic David with an aura of restrained submission.

At first, public sentiment in favor of the brothers was strong. Cloaked in the mantle of "Robin Hood graces" and endowed with handsome faces, it was difficult to believe the brothers guilty. By association, an air of "Jesse James" suaveness enhanced their image. To the day they were hanged, their family, their attorneys, and a host of well-wishers sincerely believed in their innocence (see appendix D).

The Trial and Its Aftermath

Perhaps the most intriguing phenomenon of the Nicely affair was the character and ability of the lawyers engaged for trial, both for the defense and for the prosecution. The attorneys had reputations which transcended the little county seat where they practiced law. Some had served in various capacities in Washington, D.C., and were nationally known. Retained by Anthony Nicely to defend his sons was William H. Koontz, one of Somerset's most outstanding lawyers and a noted orator. Attorney Koontz traveled extensively, speaking on behalf of the Republican Party. He also served a term in Congress, where he enjoyed a distinguished career. On the death of Thaddeus Stevens, Koontz delivered in the House of Representatives an address commemorative of the public services of the renowned statesman. Attorney Koontz also had taken a conspicuous role in the impeachment of President Andrew Johnson. Mr. Koontz earned a reputation for being an outstanding public speaker, one of the finest in western Pennsylvania. His numerous speeches received repeated compliments and were noted for their high literary merit. His connection with important trials had been constant since his admission to the bar. In 1869, he built what later became known as "the judge's residence," next to the Somerset Courthouse on Union Street, and furnished it largely through Wanamakers in Philadelphia (*The Twentieth Century Bench and Bar of Pennsylvania*, 1903, II:1186-88).

Assisting Attorney Koontz was Alexander H. Coffroth, founder of the Somerset County Bar Association and a prominent representative of the Democratic Party. Also recognized as one of the strongest attorneys in the county, he had been president of the Somerset County Bar Association since its organization. Like Attorney Koontz, he engaged in most of the important cases heard before the Somerset

County Court. Before the Civil War, Coffroth was a major general of volunteers, and was affectionately addressed by his military title. In 1862, he had been elected by his party as a representative in Congress and returned again in 1878. He was the only democrat chosen to be a pallbearer for Abraham Lincoln (*The Twentieth Century Bench and Bar of Pennsylvania*, 1903, II, 1199-2000).

Also retained by the Nicelys was William Henry Ruppel. He had studied under General Coffroth, and became Coffroth's partner when admitted to the bar. Ruppel likewise was considered one of the soundest lawyers in the county, having participated in numerous civil and criminal cases with marked success (1189).

Frederick W. Biesecker, District Attorney, represented the Commonwealth. As gifted as his worthy opponents, his two most publicized trials would be the prosecution of the Nicely brothers and the McCellandtown Gang (1202).

Francis J. Kooser also was for the prosecution. Attorney Kooser had taken part in previous well-known cases to which would be added the conviction of the Nicely brothers and a later trial of the same nature, the Roddy brothers. He subsequently received unanimous endorsement for president judge in 1890 (1188).

Samuel U. Trent, a previous Somerset resident, returned from Pittsburgh, where he enjoyed a successful career with the law firm of James S. Young, Esq., to assist the prosecution. Attorney Trent was active in the successful presidential campaign of James A. Garfield. A gifted and dynamic speaker, he was noted for the fluency of his political speeches (284-86).

However, of the illustrious counsel for both the defense and the prosecution, John Cessna of Bedford was the most colorful and cosmopolitan. Representing the prosecution, his unique background bears more than superficial mention. The Cessnas frequently are mentioned in colonial records. John Cessna was a lineal fifth generation descendent of his namesake, Huguenot John Cessna. John III, his great-grandfather, was even more prestigious and notorious than his striking great-grandson. The elder Cessna was a devout patriot and epicure of colonial distinction and a delegate to the 1774 Constitutional Convention prior to the Revolution. He was twice married. His first wife died when he was seventy years of age. They had reared thirteen children. John III then married a younger woman who bore him five more children. John V, one of the prosecutors of the Nicely brothers, was six years a member of the House of Representatives and Speaker of the House from 1851 to 1863. He also served several terms in the state House of Representatives. Active in the Republican Party, he was a noted orator and enjoyed a commanding expertise as a prosecuting attorney. Upright and public-spirited, he could not fail to win the confidence and regard of his constituency. He became president of the Board of Trustees of Franklin and Marshall College, Lancaster, Pennsylvania, where he remained until the time of his death (*The Twentieth Century Bench and Bar of Pennsylvania*, 1903, II, 284-86). "Doubtless there was no public man in the state of Pennsylvania who had not met John Cessna in many state conventions, nor any of note in the nation who have not met him at national conventions, where he was always a prominent figure. His parliamentary skill and wisdom frequently guided those bodies quietly and softly to peace, good will and harmony" (Waterman 1884, 211; cf. *Biographical Dictionary of the American Congress*, 1884, I, 89).

Such an array of counsel on both sides promised the trial to be a battle of legal giants. So it appeared in the minds of the press and public. Small town journalists of the late nineteenth century were more gifted in hyperbole than comparable writers of our present age. However, the attorneys for the defense and prosecution were men of exceptional talent and expertise. Unfortunately, throughout the Nicely brothers' murder trial the eloquence of the legal giants was bogged down with trivialities and mundane court procedures. Their legal expertise was lost on an unconscious mind set that had placed an aura of guilt upon the brothers even before the trial began. It worsened the closer the day of their hanging approached. Subsequent events would prove why.

A fateful incident occurred that furthered public outrage and gradually turned what favorable opinion remained against the brothers. While awaiting the Nicely trial, the community again was stunned. This time by the robbery and inhuman torture of Christian Yoder by the notorious McCellandtown Gang on the evening of April 13, just a month and a half after the Umberger murder (see appendix B). The almost immediate capture of members of the gang in Fayette County on April 28, and their incarceration in the Somerset County jail, kept excitement and curiosity at record levels. The jailhouse became enveloped with mystery and abounded with tall tales, many of which became fact in the minds of the curious. Were the Nicely brothers members of the McCellandtown Gang, or any other gang of robbers for that matter? Would they be rescued some night by a posse from Ligonier? The Nicely brothers' murder trial was a legend before it began. Excitement would reach fever pitch as the days moved closer to the opening of the May term of the Somerset Court.

The trial began on May 30. No other prison trial in the history of the county had been so largely attended. No one previously tried created the same intense excitement and strong feeling. Ironically, the general belief was that, despite its melodramatic aspects, no case was ever more cautiously, intelligently or impartially tried (*Somerset Herald* 1889, 31 May). The courtroom filled early with people who came from all parts of the state. Spectators packed every space. Those who could not find a seat stood in the rear or along the sides of the courtroom.

The Honorable William J. Baer served as president judge. Both defendants entered pleas of not guilty. Defense attorneys requested that the brothers be tried together. At the opening of the trial neither man evidenced any special emotion or nervousness. Both presented themselves neatly dressed in newly purchased suits, their faces cleanly shaved, looking very different from the popular image associated with them. David appeared in a dark flannel shirt with sack coat and low collar. Joseph wore a black diagonal cutaway coat, high vest and high standing collar. His hair was closely clipped, his boots highly polished and a large watch chain ornamented his vest. Both were well-groomed and presented a "most genteel appearance" (*Somerset Herald* 1889, 31 May).

In opening arguments, attorneys for the defendants attempted to prove that they were victims of a conspiracy that schemed for their ultimate conviction. All evidence was circumstantial. The tracks in the snow could not have been made by the boots in evidence. The testimonies of witnesses for the Commonwealth were not reliable— based either on prejudice or dislike for the defendants. The coat and hat in evidence had been doctored for the trial. The pocketbook was not the one taken from the Nicelys when their homes were searched. The precise actions of Joseph and David on the day and night of February 27 would be corroborated by credible witnesses. Each of the accused would testify that he had been at home all that day.

Attorney Kooser, in his summary before the jury, agreed with counsel for the defense in stating that they were all a part of an important trial, perhaps the most important trial ever tried in the county, and in noting that the Umberger name was now known over all the land because of the peculiar brutality of the murder and the magnitude of the sum of money secured.

During the course of the proceedings little mention was made of the disastrous Johnstown flood either in the Somerset papers or local conversations. Everyone was so involved with the murder trial that thought was given to little else. Due to an almost fractured means of communication and the involvement of Somerset citizens in the trial, the Johnstown flood was viewed simply as a "startling rumor." While most persons in and out of the Somerset County courtroom hotly debated the outcome of the trial, the "startling rumor" began to become a stark reality. It was traced to a report received from Pittsburgh. The old feeder dam at South Fork had burst with an immense volume of water forced down the valley of the Conemaugh, carrying death and destruction in its path. Johnstown was said to be completely inundated. A further report claimed that over three hundred lives had been lost. Since the telegraph lines were down no one was able to verify the rumor (*Somerset Herald* 1889, 1 June). It would be some time later that the full extent of the Johnstown tragedy would become known. Sharp focus riveted on the courthouse. The trial of the Nicely brothers would continue for nine more days.

For the prosecution, an array of witnesses contradicted statements made by witnesses for the defense and positively identified the brothers as seen on the road leading to Jennerstown. One, Lou W. Vaneer, a bright looking, neatly dressed young man testified that he saw them on what was called the "Sand Flat" on the Laurel Mountain coming east on February 27 (*Somerset Herald* 1889, 2 April). Ella Stern positively identified Joseph Nicely as the Small Man. All questions directed to her were answered calmly and with straightforward frankness. The same could be said for Nancy Umberger.

However, the trial reached its climax with a star witness who would be long remembered. In association with the trial, the ten-year-old granddaughter of Nancy Umberger would become known as "Little Nannie Horner." Her presence and assuredness as she was questioned brought the trial to its moment of high drama.

Appearing quite calm, evidencing neither nervousness nor fright, she made a memorable appearance as she sat on the witness stand. The little girl was given a thorough cross-examination by General Coffroth, senior counsel for the defense. He failed to elicit the slightest contradiction in her testimony. She described in minute detail how both men were dressed. She was shown an overcoat found in David Nicely's home at the time of his arrest, which she identified as the coat worn by the Tall Man.

Nannie Horner was examined for several hours. Enduring the interrogation far beyond what would have been expected for a child of her age, her testimony at one point was most damaging. Holding up a coat before the witness, General Coffroth asked, "How do you know this is the coat?"

"It has a brown patch on it," was her quick response.

"But there is no patch here?"

"But the coat has two sides. Turn it around. There is the patch" (Werner 1890, 25-27).

Later, prosecutor John Cessna remarked to a reporter, "Never in the forty-seven years I have practiced law have I, in any case, civil or criminal, seen or heard a better witness in any court than this little girl" (*Somerset Herald* 1891, 2 April). Nannie Horner's testimony and John Cessna's statement were in themselves enough to highly charge an emotional climate that would bring about a guilty verdict and conviction.

John Cessna made the closing argument for the prosecution. His irresistible logic appeared to break down every barrier the defense had set up. When he had finished there was little doubt among the courtroom audience that the jury would find the defendants guilty (Werner 1890, 40).

Judge Baer finished his charge to the jury a little before seven o'clock on Friday evening, June 7. He reminded the jurors that the arguments of the brothers' counsel did not make facts, but were a discussion of the credibility of the evidence upon the guilt or innocence of the prisoners, which was entitled to due consideration. He told the jury that it could not surrender its own judgment fairly formed on all the material facts and adopt the view of the counsel.

> The evidence is solely for your consideration and from the material evidence in the case, as given by credible witnesses, you are to find the facts, and you alone are responsible for a true and faithful finding of the facts. A human life has been taken. Herman Umberger, a former citizen of this county, is dead. He was suddenly taken, without warning by persons,

whoever they were, that did not fear God, but openly and boldly served the devil and imbued their hands in his blood at the hazard of their souls (Werner 1890, 40-49).

A short time after the jurors reached their room a ballot was taken. Nine were in favor of a verdict of guilt and three voted for acquittal. At a later hour another ballot was taken, which stood eleven for conviction and one for acquittal. Next morning, just before the jury entered the courtroom, a final ballot was taken resulting in the unanimous verdict for conviction (Werner 1890, 49; cf. Somerset *Standard* 1891, 7 June). When the jury[5] returned to the courtroom, both defendants were found guilty of murder in the first degree. The motion for a new trial was argued on August 13 and 14. On August 19, Judge Baer overruled the motion for a new trial. The same day District Attorney Biesecker made a motion for the immediate sentencing of the prisoners, both of whom were condemned to death by hanging.

The relatives of the brothers, lodging and waiting at the Somerset House, received the fateful news with undue shock and surprise. Their unwavering belief in the innocence of Joseph and David and confidence in their counsel was such that they were unprepared for the severity of the verdict. However, the brothers' fate was sealed and an ominous shadow forever cast over the Nicely name. A verdict had been reached but the innocence or guilt of Joseph and David Nicely remained an open question. There followed a preposterous chain of circumstances that added to the brothers' captivating story.

The brothers remained incarcerated in the Somerset County jail. Their family and counsel persisted to the very end in efforts to bring about their freedom. Contrary to the verdict of the court and the antipathy of the general public, the brothers had sympathizers who helped make the account of their lives into legend. Support on their behalf was found on either side of the Laurel Ridge, both in Somerset and Ligonier.

The first of the intriguing circumstances took place before the trial had ended. On June 8 there appeared in the *Somerset Herald* a brief story of a well-groomed stranger who delivered a package to Squire Elijah King of Upper Turkeyfoot Township. He requested its safekeeping until the next day. When the unknown visitor failed to return, King opened the parcel and discovered a manuscript on the life of a John Beech. It included what purported to be a confession to the murder of Herman Umberger. The writer also implicated a co-conspirator named Miller.

The package contained a note asking that the manuscript be given to Anthony Nicely. Instead, King forwarded the package to Attorney Alexander H. Coffroth. The lengthy "confession" detailed the travels of John Beech through Kansas City and back to Pennsylvania via Pittsburgh, Greensburg and Johnstown. It mentioned that in Beech's travels he associated with Miller and some of Miller's friends. The latter supposedly gave Beech information about farmers in the Somerset area, including Bernard Miller near Garrett and Herman Umberger. The writer further claimed that he and Miller went to the Umberger home where Miller shot the farmer and then the two fled towards Latrobe and divided the money. He said Miller eventually went to Cumberland, Maryland, then back to Johnstown where he opened a billiard hall.

Beech wrote that he later went looking for Miller, but learned that his friend was likely among those lost in the Johnstown flood. He also indicated that while riding on a train to Greensburg he saw a woman in black identified by another passenger as the mother of the Nicely brothers. She had the saddest face he had even seen and to his last hour he would never forget the sorrow on her face. "I put off this statement as long as I could. With her look before my face, and trouble of the Nicely family, and the two boys in jail waiting to be hung, innocent. . . . I ask the justice of the peace to take a copy of this and send it to the Nicelys' family and keep a copy of it." (*Somerset Herald* 1889, 8 June).

Small credence was given to the confession of John Beech by the attorneys for the Commonwealth who reasoned that no one living in the neighborhood of Squire Elijah King had seen the confessed murderer on the Sunday of his visit or at any other time. However, the letter did hold some significance for the counsel for the defendants. What was Beech's motive in writing the confession? It was possible he could have encountered Elizabeth Nicely on the train between Ligonier and Greensburg. What would have been his reason to take the blame from the Nicely brothers? The Nicely family obtained testimony from several citizens of Fayette County that they had known a man named John Beech in Kansas, but none of them had seen him since his departure. They used this information to delay the action of the Board of Pardons, awaiting the possibility of more favorable evidence. On March 3, 1891, the Nicelys brought suit against John O. Rauch for conspiracy. The suit was dismissed after a hearing was held the following week (*Somerset Herald* 1891, 2 April). Since the Nicelys were residents of Westmoreland County they handled their legal matters in Greensburg and made numerous trips to the county seat in behalf of Joseph and David, whose next actions further divided people as to their innocence or guilt.

The Somerset jailhouse was notoriously insecure. Escapes had been made by former prisoners, and due to the notoriety of Joseph and David, a guard was kept within the jail both day and night. In spite of these precautions, on September 16, the brothers made a bold dash for their freedom and succeeded in escaping from the jail. At noon, the day watchman had gone to the town pump to fill a bucket for drinking water. On his return, Deputy Sheriff Milton McMillan unlocked the jail door from the outside and admitted him. As the guard stepped away from the door, Joseph Nicely, having managed to escape from his cell, sprang forward and pointed a revolver at the deputy. The two men struggled, and the deputy sheriff received two bullet wounds from Joseph Nicely's gun. McMillan, however, had succeeded in locking the door, but could not take the key out of the lock. David put his hand through a small opening in the door and unlocked the door, making his escape while Joseph was still struggling with Deputy Sheriff McMillan. On being shot the second time, McMillian released his hold on Joseph who ran out the front door of the jail.

In a matter of moments an alarm was raised and citizens of the town were on the scene for an immediate pursuit of the prisoners. The escapees had been seen entering the densely wooded area northeast of town known as Oak Ridge. The section was surrounded speedily and a diligent search begun. Ultimately, David Nicely was discovered, having climbed to the top of a tree. With rifles leveled at him he descended pleading that he not be lynched. As he was brought into town, an angry crowd shouted, "Lynch him! Hang him!" After David's capture, he was heard to have exclaimed, "For God's sake, don't let them lynch me. It wasn't me that did the shooting." Sometime later, Joseph Nicely was found concealed under thick growing brushes. The brothers were returned to the Somerset jail. In the assembled crowd outside the courthouse, was a Mrs. Elias Cunningham who startled Joseph with her curt remark, "You are now in the hands of the Somerset County Dutch!" (Werner 1890, 57)

Before their escape there had been some reversal of opinion and increasing sympathy for the Nicely brothers as well as increasing doubt in the minds of many as to whether they were guilty. But this desperate attempt to escape and the shooting of the deputy sheriff reversed the minds of many who had previously believed in their innocence. It became the consensus of opinion that Joseph and David Nicely were capable of killing anyone who stood in their way.

Despite the actions of the brothers, their lawyers and their parents resolutely continued to uphold their innocence. Having failed in their appeal to the Supreme Court, the lawyers resorted to pleading with the Board of Pardons. A hearing was scheduled for April 18, 1890. The opening speech in behalf of the brothers was made by William H. Koontz. In an elaborate argument, which took all of the morning session and part of the afternoon, the attorney reviewed the facts of the case and claimed it was the duty of the board to look into the whole case and to examine the evidence and the law. The hearing occupied over thirteen hours. The decision of the pardon board was adverse to the Nicely brothers and their attorneys. A second hearing was held by the pardon board on November 11, 1890. The action of the former board was upheld.

Due to its continuing reputation for being inadequate and insecure, the Somerset jail was rebuilt and remodeled during the summer of 1890. While the work was in progress, the Nicely brothers and other Somerset prisoners were taken to Indiana and confined in the Indiana county jail. On completion of the new jail in Somerset in the early fall the prisoners were returned. Hardly had the new jail been completed and Joseph and David returned when another escape was attempted. On Saturday evening, November 29, Joseph and David made a second escape attempt—especially alarming because it was from the new jail. Saws used in making their escape were believed to have been given to the brothers by friends or family members while they were being held in the Indiana jail. Thirteen bright, keen toothed steel saws measuring from five to nine inches in length, were found in the cells occupied by the Nicely brothers in the county jail. The sheriff found seven saws in David's cell, six in Joseph's.

"How much will you give us if we tell you how to grow them," asked David with a laugh. "You ought to leave us a few for seed" (*Somerset Herald* 1891, 2 April).

With the help of other prisoners, the brothers had previously sawed the heads from a number of rivets in the jail door preparatory to an escape. They had not attempted the escape sooner because they believed the Board of Pardons or the governor would interfere and prevent their execution.

Among the other prisoners was a burglar who sawed the lock from a trap door in the ceiling of his cell ten days earlier than the escape attempt. With access to the attic of the jail, the prisoner was later to confess that he went up into the loft every day where he worked on loosening the bricks in the wall. Other prisoners stood guard in case of the approach of any of the jail officials. Having managed to open each cell door and with easy access to the attic, the prisoners finally broke through the brick wall. Hastily making a rope of bed sheets and blankets, they removed the outer layer of bricks and opened a hole alongside the water spout in the northeast corner of the wall. They were prepared to make their escape. Sliding down the makeshift rope, Joseph Nicely was the first to descend. About halfway down, the rope broke. Joseph fell about ten feet to the ground resulting in painful injuries to his legs. David Nicely was the third to descend and did not appear to have known of the rope breaking. He also was badly hurt. Both brothers managed to escape. Alexander Queer, an arsonist, who was elderly and obese, was the last to descend. When he fell to the ground from the shortened rope he broke one of his legs. His moaning at the time caught the attention of someone passing by who alerted the authorities. Queer died several days later (Werner 1890, 66).

Again, an angered and armed group assembled for immediate pursuit of the escapees. A reward of five hundred dollars was offered for the return of the prisoners. Speculations were that the Nicely brothers, with assistance, would try to find their way back to their homes in Ligonier. The next day, Sunday, both sides of the Laurel Ridge were searched for the escaped prisoners. No trace of the Nicelys was found. However, the wounds of the brothers were believed to be so serious that neither would have been able to get very far. As suspected, they hid in nearby barns. David Nicely was found in the barn of William H. Ferner, a young farmer residing about one mile north of Somerset. He was brought back to the jail on Monday morning. Ferner stated that he had gone to the barn before daybreak to feed his cattle. After climbing into the hayloft and while putting forks of hay in the racks, he was startled when he heard a voice saying, "For God's sake, don't kill me; I am hurt and want to give myself up" (Werner 1890, 63). Seeing David's helplessness, Ferner assisted him into his house and prepared food for him. David complained constantly of his foot and Ferner bathed it in cold water. Notwithstanding his helpless condition, David offered Ferner $1,000 to carry him to the other side of the Laurel Mountain, double the reward that had been offered. Ferner refused the offer and returned David to the jail.

For the next twenty-four hours, the country between Somerset and the Ligonier Valley was scoured thoroughly for Joseph. Almost every barn along the several roads leading to the Pennsylvania Road over the Laurel Mountain was searched. Tuesday afternoon, Jonathan Barclay, a farmer living within half a mile of the jail drove quietly up behind the jail building in a two-horse wagon. There were two other passengers with him, William Miller, a neighbor, and a man clad in a heavy overcoat and wearing a heavy, broad-brimmed, felt hat pulled low over his forehead. It was Joseph Nicely, discovered in the Barclay barn (Werner 1890, 64–65).

"I had no idea he was in the barn," Barclay stated. "All my neighbors were searching their barns so I decided that I had better search mine." Early that afternoon, Robert Hochstetler, his seventeen-year-old helper came running down from the threshing floor and said there was someone up there and he believed it was Nicely. Barclay found Joseph sitting on a log in the mow. He was trembling and could hardly talk. As with Ferner, Barclay bathed Joseph's feet and fed him. He put his own overcoat and hat on Joseph when they started for town (Werner 1890, 64). Each of the brothers returned with a broken foot.

Even after the second attempt to escape, and despite their incredible and desperate actions, the Nicely brothers' counsel remained immovable as to their innocence. The attorneys saw the Nicelys as victims of a conspiracy, either from a robber gang to which they belonged or from people in Ligonier, some of whom bitterly disliked the Nicely brothers for one reason or another. They were sympathetic with the belief of the brothers that their only chance for freedom was by a pardon or an escape. Their case finally was carried to the highest judicial tribunal of the Commonwealth. The lawyers appeared for another hearing before Governor James Adams Beaver on January 9, 1891. Their pleas were denied. The governor signed the death warrants on January 20, the day before his term of office expired. April 2, 1891, was fixed as the date of execution.

The case of Joseph and David Nicely had been taken before the Board of Pardons four times. The first hearing was on April 18, 1890; the second, November 11, 1890; the third was a hearing before the governor on January 9, 1891; and the fourth was a motion for reargument before the new Board of Pardons on January 24, 1891. All appeals for pardon failed. Among the papers placed before the pardon board was the aforementioned confession of one John Beech (Werner 1890, 66). Among other depositions was one from John W. Beck, a juror for the case, in which he stated that he had been coerced by his fellow jurors into agreeing to a verdict of murder in the first degree (Blackburn and Wilfley 1906, 563). Finally, the parents of the brothers brought allegations of conspiracy against the officers who had made the arrest. This too was dismissed as unfounded (*Somerset Herald* 1891, 8 April).

About a month prior to the time set for the executions Joseph Nicely suddenly evidenced a mental problem. He complained of severe pains in his head and began to act in most peculiar ways. He played the role so convincingly that a local practitioner, Dr. Kimmel, a comparatively young man with a large practice but with limited knowledge of mental patients, concluded that the affliction was real. To substantiate his diagnosis, Dr. H. L. Orth of Harrisburg, a well-known expert on such cases, was brought to Somerset. He agreed with Dr. Kimmel and declared Joseph insane[6] (Werner, 71).

Again, the Nicely lawyers submitted an appeal for executive clemency. Again it was denied, this time by the new governor, Robert Emory Pattison. Governor Pattison's position was that the visit of Dr. Orth had not been at his direction. Therefore, the governor took no action on the application for the respite of the murderers and was not likely to interfere with the execution of the death warrant. Evidence of Joseph Nicely's insanity was not sufficiently conclusive to justify staying the executions, and as to the guilt of the Nicely brothers, nothing had been produced to convince the governor that they had been wrongly convicted (Werner 1890, 72). When Joseph was made aware of the situation, he quickly became rational. As a result, little doubt was left in the minds of the authorities as to his guilt. Governor Pattison upheld the death warrant of Governor Beaver for April 2, death by hanging.

As the weeks moved closer to the day of execution, Somerset was filled with rumors that the Nicely brothers would be rescued before April 2. As an extraordinary precaution an outside guard was placed around the jail. Anonymous telegrams were received by the sheriff warning that an effort would be made to set the brothers free. As late as the evening of April 1, a telegram was received by Attorney F. J.

Kooser stating that a large armed posse had left Ligonier and was headed in the direction of Somerset. Four additional guards were put on duty during the night. However, no effort was made to storm the Somerset jail (Werner 1890, 71).

Death by Hanging

Nowhere in the evolution of our society is there a more complex phenomenon than the death penalty (Teeters 1963, 24). Early English customs included unbelievable sacrificial rituals, such as drawing and quartering, pressing with stones, burning at the stake, and hanging. Such laws were supported by practically all men of the day. The literary classic often mentioned as a vivid description of these macabre occurrences is William Thackeray's "Going to See a Man Hanged" as published in *Fraser's Magazine* in 1850 (Teeters 1963, 24).

Throughout the nineteenth century, some European countries had already abolished capital punishment. Yet in England, public hangings remained a kind of officially sanctioned "Witches Sabbath" (Koestler 1970, 179-80). As late as 1864, the *Times* described a crowd assembled to watch a hanging: "Before the slight slow vibrations of the body had well ended, robbery and violence, loud laughing, oaths and obscene conduct reigned round the gallows." In 1807, a crowd of forty thousand became so crazed at an execution that nearly a hundred dead and dying were lying in the street (Koestler 1970, 179-80).

Not only the lower classes were affected. Grandstands were erected for distinguished onlookers. Balconies and windows in the vicinity brought fabulous prices from viewers. Ladies, wearing black Venetian masks, queued to pay last visits to the condemned man in his cell. Many traveled anywhere in the country to see a good hanging. The governor of Newgate Prison habitually entertained distinguished viewers after an execution for breakfast (Koestler 1970, 179-80).

Up to the nineteenth century public hanging had been popular in the early American colonies. Like Great Britain, capital punishment often meant the hanging of victims by the neck until dead. It was the most common form of execution. Reprieves and pardons were common and often melodramatically timed to be announced at the very last moment at the gallows (Newman 1976, 144-45). Yet, colonial hangings were of a different nature than those in England. Although they were still enjoyed as a spectacle, the behavior around the gallows was more orderly. Nor was it the scene of delirium as was often found in London. A sermon preached by an officiating minister was taken seriously, and hymns were solemnly sung as the offender was sent on his way. In contrast to the English practice that published the criminal's confession, the American practice was to publish the accompanying minister's sermon, usually charged with strong Calvinistic overtones of "hellfire and damnation."

The first book published in Boston was a sermon preached by Increase Mather at a public hanging in 1675, entitled, *The Wicked Man's Portion*. In 1787, Benjamin Rush published a paper denouncing public executions, and by the 1830s many states began to conduct their executions inside prison walls (Newman 1978, 144-45). New England and the Quaker colonies of Pennsylvania and New Jersey had a more humane sét of criminal punishments than prevailed in New York and in the South. In Massachusetts, barbarous or inhumane tortures were forbidden almost from the beginning. However, the puritan code leaned in the direction of exemplary and humiliating punishments such as the ducking stool[7] for dishonest tradesmen, the stocks for the vagrant, the letter "A" sewn on the garment for the adulterer, branding for the burglar, or riding a wooden horse with an empty pitcher in one hand to indicate a propensity to strong drink. Hanging was the normal method of capital punishment, and it was by this method, not by burning, that the New England witches were executed. In Pennsylvania, murder alone was punishable by death (Matthews 1962, 779-80).

With the adoption of the Constitution, hanging remained the sole legal means of capital punishment until the innovation of electrocution and the use of lethal gas (Andrews, Dictionary of American History 1976, III:249). Notwithstanding the provision in the Constitution and some changes from the British tradition, hangings continued to be cruel and macabre affairs. A body often was left suspended for an entire day. Methods of execution continued to be excruciating and severe. The victim frequently was flung from a ladder, or placed on a cart that was wheeled out from under him. Instead of a quick, painless death, the sufferer endured the agonies of slow strangulation (Teeters 1963, 24; cf. Trombley 1991, 9, 13). Most victims were taken from the jail in a cart accompanied by one or more ministers and by those officials who were required to attend. Among the condemned, some sat on their coffins while others stood or walked before or behind the cart. Generally the criminals were blindfolded with their hands shackled. The nineteenth century brought about more humane principles in America. The scaffold was established and the hangman's knot developed, the combined effect of both created a snapping of the spinal column that resulted in a swift and less painful end (Teeters 1963, 24).

When executions were still public events, they held enormous interest. Perhaps no single event brought more spectators in those years than a public hanging. People drove for miles to be present; some camped in the vicinity for several days. Such a gathering of people naturally brought camp followers as entertainers, vendors, pickpockets, promoters, evangelists, sightseers, peddlers, and medicine men. After the Civil War, executions began to be performed in the jail yard or at a state penitentiary. With the passing of public execution went the carnival spirit which prevailed when thousands viewed a hanging (McDade 1961, xxx-xxxi). The form of gallows and the method of hanging changed gradually. Yet a curious interest in what took place at the gallows remained. As with the Nicely Brothers, a regular scaffold was provided indoors, with a trapdoor for dropping the prisoner through the floor. The drop in this manner, with the rope close under the prisoner's ear, produced a dislocation of the neck that rendered him unconscious immediately (*Greensburg Morning Rview* march 23, 1891).

The decorum of those who went to their death on the gallows varied from cowardly groveling to superb stoicism. Many seemed indifferent to their fate, some contemptuous of the occasion, even a few were lighthearted. William Crawford, executed at Washington, Pennsylvania, in February 1823, held nothing but contempt for the courts, including the judge, jury, witnesses, and even his own relatives. On his way to the gallows he peeled and ate an apple and actually told the accompanying minister to "mind his own business," when asked if he wished to have prayers said for him (McDade 1961, II:8-9). The majority of the condemned, however, were sober, prayerful, and fully conscious of the solemnity of the occasion (Teeters 1963, II:25). Records show that 252 persons had been hanged publicly in the Commonwealth of Pennsylvania from 1682 to 1837, before the state became the first to abolish public hangings (II:v).

The atmosphere surrounding public hangings gradually changed from colonial solemnity to extravagant festival. The scenes encircling the hangings frequently were degrading and disgraceful; occasions for large hilarious gatherings, mostly bent on idle curiosity. There was usually the fear of some attempt to rescue the prisoner. Onlookers came by wagons, horseback or on foot. The procession continued in constantly increasing proportions right up to the moment of the execution. Many came long distances, arriving the night before and crowding the taverns, or sleeping in the wagons in which they had arrived. On the road to the place of execution, booths were erected for the sale of food and beverages. The presence of the military often was required to prevent riots or the possible rescue of the condemned (II: 25).

The first murder in New England was committed in 1630 with a gun. The ax would appear to be no less lethal a weapon in the eighteenth and nineteenth centuries. The tool was within easy reach in every household, and there is a long list of murders of not only one person but of whole families that were committed with axes. Even at the end of the nineteenth century, when firearms had become quite common, Lizzie Borden's parents demise proclaimed the preeminence of the ax as a weapon of destruction. Arsenic was most commonly used poison, outnumbering all other poisons eight to one. It was procurable at a pharmacy or a hardware store and the time-honored and hackneyed reason given for its purchase was "for rats" (McDade 1961, xix).

An early case of "arsenic and old lace," was that of Mrs. Martha Grinder of Allegheny County. There is no way of knowing how many persons may have been the victims of her coy antics. She was a confirmed arsenic poisoner, "a motherly person bent on doing good." Many of the recipients of her favors became ill. Some died. Finally a bride and groom moved next to her home. Befriended with food prepared by Martha, the young Mrs. Crothers became ill and returned to her mother's home where she eventually died. An autopsy showed traces of arsenic poisoning. Martha was convicted of murder and went to the scaffold on January 19, 1866. She was especially calm during her stay in jail awaiting execution. Apparently she had no "qualms of conscious" concerning her acts. She appeared worried only at one point: Would she look nice when she went to the gallows? (McDade 1961, II:8)

At the last public execution in Philadelphia on May 19, 1837, nineteen-year-old James Morgan was hanged at the corner of Twelfth and Spring Garden Streets, in the presence of some 20,000 persons, following his conviction for piracy and murder. The John Lechler hanging at Lancaster on October 25, 1822, drew a crowd of between 20,000 and 30,000 persons. The square leading from the jail to the place of execution "was a solid mass and when the procession arrived at the spot it appeared to be already occupied by a body of people more numerous than those advancing" (McDade 1961, xix). Wrote one person concerning the consequences in Lancaster on the night of the execution, "Fifteen persons were committed to prison, one for murder and one for larceny, the rest for vagrancy having no doubt been attracted to the scene through prevailing curiosity" (77). Charles Bindle in his autobiography describes the execution of a young soldier named William Welch. Accused and convicted of burglary, the Supreme Executive Council refused to intercede and he was executed on July 17, 1784. Bindle stated that fifteen to twenty thousand men, women and children attended, completely covering the hillside near the gallows. He wrote: "An old woman walked nearly seventy miles to see the execution. Being fatigued, a little before the execution, she fell asleep and did not wake up until it was over, when she cried most bitterly" (28).

Edward Livingston, a lawyer, reported an orgy at Orwigsburg, Schuylkill County in 1824. Thousands of people had gathered to witness an execution that did not take place. The crowd grew impatient as the execution was delayed and "raised a ferocious cry." When a last minute reprieve was granted to the victim due to insanity, "their fury knew no bounds and the poor maniac was snatched by the officers of justice from the fate which the most violent among them seemed determined to inflict" (McDade 1961, 26).

Somerset County was not without its legends and accompanying superstitions resulting from former hangings. About fifteen persons had been tried for murder prior to the execution of the Nicely brothers. In all but two cases the murderers were hanged. Two of the most spectacular and sensational were the earliest. The first concerns a German by the name of Caracas Spangenberg who posed as a German reformed missionary. Spangenberg was a native of Hesse, and came to America with the mercenaries whom the British brought from that country in 1776 to assist in the Revolutionary War. At the close of the war he decided to remain after the colonies had gained their independence. He sought admission to the ministry of the German Reformed Church, but the Philadelphia conference, after examining his case, rejected him. The following year Spangenberg renewed his application and again was turned down. An uncle, the Rev. Samuel Dubbendorff, finally interceded for Spangenberg's ordination and he was accepted.

The young minister located near Selingsgrove, but soon aroused doubts as to his credibility. He won the affection of a respectable young woman whom he courted and to whom he proposed marriage. The day before the wedding it was learned that the minister had a wife and family in Europe. Forced to leave Selingsgrove, he attempted to bury his past and became pastor of a small congregation near Chambersburg. His true character again was exposed and he was forced to move on to Bedford and finally to Berlin, then in Bedford County. Again his conduct caused much displeasure, but he managed to remain despite many complaints and protests. The congregation was divided on the subject and it finally was agreed that the members should assemble at the church on March 19, 1795, to settle the matter. Spangenberg was present for the occasion.

Jacob Glassmore, a prominent and influential member of the church and reputedly a man of unimpeachable character, remained silent until the vote was about to be taken. He then rose and spoke strongly in favor of a change of ministers. When the speaker finished, Spangenberg sprang to his feet livid with rage. He drew a knife and struck Glassmore. Glassmore immediately died while a stunned congregation stood motionless in horror. Spangenberg was arrested and immediately confined in jail. The jury before whom he was tried brought in a verdict of guilty of murder in the first degree. On October 11, 1795, he was taken in a wagon, seated on his coffin, to a scaffold erected in the town commons where he was hanged (Koontz 1906, 415-17).

The second, a darkly curious and oddly romantic affair, previously was mentioned with reference to how the Black Horse Inn got its name. Accounts vary as to who the victim was, a traveling young doctor or a drover, yet surviving research points strongly to the former. Both accounts, however, record the presence at the inn of a doctor, a drover and two Frenchmen. On a winter's night, January 27, 1807, the Frenchmen arrived in a sleigh at the tavern on the summit of the Allegheny Mountain. They spoke in broken English, said they were strangers to the country who were traveling for pleasure. Such elegantly dressed gentlemen seldom had been seen in the tavern. Handsomely mannered and dressed, the taller and elder of the two possessed striking features; jet black hair and piercing dark eyes. The younger was described as being of a slight build, pale, intellectual in appearance, with large, soft brown eyes and chestnut hair.

Among the drinkers at the bar was a drover named Pollock (Werner 1890, III:1). He not only drank too much but was verbose about his exploits as an itinerant cattle salesman. Having irritated most of the assembled men by his boisterous manner, all were relieved when he rode away on his horse a little before dusk. Soon after, the Frenchmen inquired as to where the next good stopping place was to be found. They ordered their horse and sleigh and drove away in the tracks of the drover. Likewise, the doctor followed on his unusually handsome and regal black horse. The next morning the doctor's body was found with a bullet through his brain. The Frenchmen were suspected, pursued and found at a tavern some miles beyond. The older of the two attempted to escape but was apprehended and killed. The younger was taken to Somerset and tried for the murder of the doctor. The young Frenchman vehemently protested his innocence, as well as that of his dead companion. He wore a miniature, set with pearls, of a lovely woman. Giving his name as Noel Hugel, he was hung from a tree in the Somerset cemetery. His remains were interred by the side of the public road. The doctor's riderless horse wildly roamed the mountains, and the inn inherited its name, the Black Horse Inn.

A legend grew that Noel Hugel was the tragic victim of circumstantial evidence and the true murderer of the doctor escaped. No one thought to place suspicion on the drover. Hugel was believed by many to be an innocent man. He never was accounted for, having been refused the privilege of writing to relatives in France (*Somerset Democrat* 1891, 1 April; cf. Baldwin 1964, 49). Many years after the hanging, a party of young men were jovially discussing Noel Hugel. A dispute arose over where the Frenchman was buried. His grave site was discovered and his remains exhumed within a few feet of the spot where the execution took place (Werner 1890, III:2).

In 1896, four years after the hanging of David and Joseph Nicely, two brothers, James and John Roddy, were found guilty of the murder of David Berkey. The Roddy brothers were the last in the county to be hanged prior to electrical execution. The murder bears many striking similarities to that of Herman Umberger. Committed seven years later, Berkey was an affluent farmer who made his home with his wife and daughter in northern Somerset County. Respected by friends and neighbors for his integrity, he was known to have kept a sizable sum of money in his home and therefore was a target for robbery. The brothers tied their victim, tortured him by applying candles to his feet, then killed him. They left the scene of the crime on horses stolen from one of the tenants. Eventually, the brothers were found and charged with murder and the case was brought to trial. The jury reached a verdict of first degree murder. The brothers were executed together on April 26, 1898 (Teeters 1963, II:9-10). Like the Nicely brothers, they denied their guilt to the very end. Somerset County thus would gain the ill-fated distinction of having committed two sets of brothers to the gallows. There were three sets of brothers executed in public hangings in Pennsylvania prior to 1834: John and Walter Winter, Chester County, July 3, 1728, for the murder of Toke Collie of French Creek; Michael and Patrick Burne, Philadelphia, December 9, 1747, for burglary; and Benjamin and James Nugent, Cumberland County, June 17, 1780, for highway robbery.

From 1834 to 1906, five pairs of brothers were executed privately or within county jails. The Nicelys and the Roddys were among this group. The others included Blaise and Matthias Skupiski, Polish immigrants of Philadelphia who were accused of murdering a young jewelry peddler named Jacob Lehman. The young victim's body was discovered under the ice of the Delaware River by children who were playing in the area. Blaise, who probably knew nothing of the felony's plot, was executed on December 3, 1852. Matthias, who masterminded the sordid crime and probably had an unknown accomplice, was hanged on August 6.

The second pair of brothers executed were Jonathan and Uriah Mooyer of Snyder County. They were members of a foursome that robbed and murdered an elderly couple, John and Gretchen Kintzler, who lived on Jack's Mountain near Truxelville, on December 2, 1877. Jonathan was executed at Middleburg on March 24, 1882; Uriah on March 7, 1883. As with the Nicely brothers, the Kintzler murders became a Snyder County saga.

The third pair of brothers condemned to die were Bigler and Charles Johnson of Bradford County. They were convicted of the murder of Bigler's estranged wife, Maggie. Disgruntled over having to pay Maggie, twenty years his senior, support money, Bigler and his brother killed Maggie and her ten-year-old niece, Annie

Benjamin. Bigler was executed on July 25, 1905, and his brother Charles was executed two years later (Teeters 1963, II:9-10).

The Brothers' Final Days

The days immediately before the execution of Joseph and David Nicely were filled with raw nerved anticipation and the wildest of rumors concerning their escape. Anthony Nicely, the prisoners' father, arrived in Somerset the Monday prior to the execution, still seeking a reprieve for his sons. He was seen, accompanied by one of his attorneys, A. H. Coffroth, visiting the sheriff's office where he asked for four passes to the hanging.

To further complicate the already seriously convoluted affair, a letter arrived addressed to the sheriff making the claim that two peddlers were responsible for the crime. The *Greensburg Daily Tribune* for Monday, March 23, reported that the counsel for the prosecution had received a letter from a credible resident of Ligonier warning that an attempt would be made by friends to rescue the brothers, "If they conclude not to attack the jail they will certainly endeavor to blow it up with dynamite."

The excitement and interest in the Nicely brothers grew more intense with each hour that brought the condemned men closer to the gallows. The number of requests for passes to witness the execution was beyond control. Sheriff Good had on file 500 applications for admission, which included reporters, sheriffs, detective and police officers from at least fifteen different states. Several artists and photographers arrived drawing and taking pictures of the jailhouse and surrounding points and places of interest. Railroads arranged for special trains. Everything and everyone seemed to be enveloped in sentimentality and sensationalism that bordered on the irrational. The reality was, however, that on Saturday, March 28, a telegram arrived from Harrisburg with the final decision of the governor that the execution would take place on Thursday, April 2 (*Greensburg Daily Tribune* 1891, 23 March; cf. Werner 1890, 72).

In an unusual turn of events, just hours before the execution, David gave a written confession to his spiritual advisor, Elder Granger of the Disciples' Church.

Although the brothers had maintained their innocence throughout their long ordeal, David now stated in his confession that he was present the night Herman Umberger was murdered. But his confession stipulated a rather striking **condition.** He was not the one who killed Herman Umberger. He further stated that he had a pistol, but fired into the ceiling intending only to frighten the Umbergers. He claimed that he left his home on February 27, 1889, to go to Somerset County intent on robbery, but not murder. The April 8 *Somerset Herald* reported that the following confession was made by David Nicely to Elder C.W. Granger on Wednesday, April 1, 1891. The statement was recorded as David spoke. David placed his signature to the document in a firm, bold hand. Shortly after making and signing the statement, he was baptized by immersion by Elder Granger and received the Sacrament of Communion.

Somerset Jail,
Somerset, Pa. April 1, 1891.

My evidence in court was not true in this: I said I was not present at Herman Umbergers when I was. The pocketbook produced in court as mine was not the one I gave Will Thomas, as I testified in court. It was bogus.

Hamilton Smith's testimony in the case against me was false in this: I was not in Ligonier on the 27 day of February as he swore.

Lew Beener and Ed McCraken did not meet me on the pike, as they stated in court.

Charles Vaneer and Lewis Veneer, his son, could not have recognized me where their testimony says they did, on the Pittsburgh and Philadelphia Pike, February 27, 1889.

I make these statements in view of approaching execution, in the fear of God, truthfully, to C.W. Granger, my spiritual advisor.

David C. Nicely

The wording in his confession would lead one to believe that he had received instructions from someone else, perhaps a member of the gang. In his statement David makes no reference to his brother nor does he say that it was Joseph who was with him in the Umberger home. David's late confession raises the question as to whether Joseph was present the night of the murder. The implication of David's confession is that he was not. Could David's accomplice have been someone other than Joseph? Another member of a robber gang to which the Nicely brothers belonged? Was the actual murderer of Herman Umberger another member of the gang? Why did David not name his brother?

Joseph Nicely made no public confession. He was, however, counseled by the Rev. A. J. Beal of the Evangelical Association. At one time he had been a member of that denomination. There was a general belief that Joseph did make some sort of a confession, as he sent for Mr. Beal on the morning of April 2. The minister would neither affirm nor deny whether a confession had been made.

Though their faces and bodies visibly portrayed the strain of their long ordeal and though public opinion had turned strongly against them, both David and Joseph possessed personal traits and winsomeness that made, not only their lawyers, but some of their sharpest accusers, continue to question their guilt. A Somerset newspaper reported that Joseph was gifted with a particularly fine high tenor voice. Having once taught singing, during the first year of his imprisonment he made the walls of the old jail resound with his singing. A resident of the Ligonier Valley recalled in his mid-nineties that as a boy of four, he heard Joseph sing in a church choir. One of the vivid memories of his childhood was the sadness he felt when he learned that Joseph Nicely had been hanged.[8]

On the other hand, Joseph Nicely undoubtedly had a somewhat checkered career. Early in life, he was involved in a number of crimes. Believed to have spent a summer with the Jesse James gang, he also was imprisoned in Ohio for impersonating a detective and wanted in that state for burning barns of well-to-do farmers. Though his father was an established resident of the Ligonier Valley and widely respected, both David and Joseph's reputations caused them to be feared by neighboring families. Many thefts that were committed among the local farmers were attributed to the brothers.

The content of folklore can involve distortions of history as has been the case with culturally transmitted images of crime. The widespread interpretation of the outlaw as hero is a typical example. It applies to the James as well as the Nicely brothers. The Nicelys were related to the James brothers. Their mother Elizabeth, a daughter of Daniel James, was a cousin of the father of Jesse and Frank James. Joseph was believed at one time to have been a member of the James gang. After his return from the west he frequently boasted of his relationship with the James brothers. David named his youngest son Jesse James (*Greensburg Daily Tribune* 1891, 2 April). David and Joseph Nicely patterned their lives after their more notorious western relatives with the exception of being rank amateurs in their ominous deeds. Newspaper accounts of the murder and their two escapes made them into the dangerous desperadoes they were not. One cannot help but wonder why they were so engaged when a part of their lives would place them in more conventional circumstances.

The fateful April 2 arrived. By 8:00 A.M., Sheriff Good had received several telegrams warning him to be on guard as a host of supporters of the Nicelys were on their way to rescue them. This caused considerable uneasiness among the officials and the guard at the jail. Already troubled, the concerns of the jail officials increased. A crowd began to accumulate around the jail house as dawn began to break.

About 11:00 A.M., the unrelenting counsel, Messrs. Coffroth, Koontz and Rupel, called on the brothers. They first met with Joseph alone who continued to profess his innocence. He contended that fraud and perjury had placed him where he was. He further stated that many testimonies made against him simply were not true. Men and women falsely testified in order to get the reward that was offered (Werner 1890, 79). Sheriff McMillan entered Joseph's cell that morning. Joseph grasped his hand and led him to the rear of the cell and begged forgiveness for the wounds and suffering he had caused the deputy. Joseph contended he had every intention of making reparations for the expense and suffering he had caused the sheriff. The deputy assured him of his full forgiveness. General Koontz remarked that from the very start the brothers had been urged to tell the unqualified truth in this matter. He further stated that he believed the whole story had not been told (*Somerset Herald* 1891, 8 April).

About 12:45 P.M. the brothers were joined by Elder Granger and the Rev. Beal for a final service of worship. It was the understanding between them that their final spiritual experience would be shared. Joseph made a fervent prayer. David was at first kneeling with his back to the others but in the midst of Joseph's prayer he turned and placed his arms around his brother. Joseph would die proclaiming his innocence. Joseph's last letter to his wife was published on the morning of his execution.[9] His prison diary, which surfaced in 1988 and is now property of the Somerset County Historical Museum, contains statements that affirm his innocence. An unpublished letter from Joseph to wife was found along with the diary asserting the same. Despite the unsavory side to his life, Joseph's diaries and his unpublished letters to his wife evidence a spiritual nature that was not a part of his public image. David 's confession showed that he was present the night Herman Umberger was killed. A striking part of his confession records that when he left his home on February 27, 1889, it was to go to Somerset County for robbery, but not murder. He makes no reference in any way to Joseph, nor does he say who it was that went with him to the Umberger home (Werner 1890, 72–73).

April 2 proved to be a most disagreeable day. From early morning, a mixture of rain and snow fell almost continuously. As past hangings had proved, inclement weather did not deter the morbidly curious from descending on Somerset from all parts of the state. Though not to be a public affair, people arrived by train and wagon; on horseback as well as on foot. One odd but enlightened individual who had himself traveled a distance of fifteen miles was known to have remarked, "I believe all the fools in the state are here today" (Werner 1890, 75).

As the morning turned to high noon an uneasy anxiety swept through the gathering spectators. The belief grew stronger, though more imaginative than factual, that a rescue party would reach Somerset and make a desperate effort to free the brothers.[10] Yet a curious impact of a different kind was laid on the already strained situation. The defendants' counsel, the night before, received a telegram from Governor Pattison stating conclusively that he could not interfere in the execution. All hopes for a reprieve were vanquished. Considering the cloud that hung over the few true believers, and the sharp-edged, raw-nerved judgments of every street witness; eyes were focused on the county jail. A general melee was a possibility.

The *Somerset Herald*, in its April 2, 1891 issue, carried an etching depicting seats arranged on both the upper and lower corridors of the jail house. As nothing could be seen or heard by those in the lower corridor until after the trap had fallen and then only the lower part of the victims' bodies could be seen, the majority of those admitted tried to crowd into the upper corridor. Demands made on Sheriff Good for tickets to view the hanging continued until the time of the execution. Sixty tickets were issued (Teeters 1963, 117-18; cf. Blackburn and Welfley

1906, II). Outside, for a space of about twenty-five feet surrounding the jail building, the crowd surged toward the walls.

Death warrants were read to both prisoners. Local newspapers reported the final moments of the brothers to the most minute detail. They were led to the trap doors. Their hands were fastened behind by handcuffs. Nooses were passed over their heads and drawn up to fit their necks with the knot behind. Black hoods were drawn over their heads and tied about their necks with drawstrings. It was the legal responsibility of the county sheriff to perform the onerous task, which in colonial days was delegated to professional executioners who often were masked and sometimes hideously disguised. The brothers Joseph and David Nicely, age forty-two and twenty-seven respectively, were hanged in the Somerset County jail at 1:43 P.M. April 2, 1891, by Sheriff Isaiah Good (*Somerset Herald* 1891, 2 April).[11]

One great advantage the Somerset jail had over all other prisons in the state was that, as a result of recent remodeling, the gallows in use was superior in mechanism and structure. The beamthat supported the ropes, the rings through which they were thrust, the two death traps, the lever for releasing the traps, were in such condition it was not necessary for the sheriff to conduct the number of tests made in other jails (*Somerset Herald* 1891, 8 April).

When the brothers were pronounced dead and their bodies lowered, they were taken into the sheriff's office. C. A. Lowry, a mortician from Ligonier, partially embalmed them and placed their bodies in coffins. As they were carried from the jail, thousands lined to view the coffins. Newspapers nationally carried accounts of the trial and execution. After a journey of some eight hours in a downpour of rain, the long day ended as the cortege reached Ligonier about 11:00 P.M. that night.

In addition to the Nicely brothers, the Somerset jail held as prisoners members of the infamous McCellandtown gang, inmates found guilty and sentenced to long terms of imprisonment for robbing and brutally torturing Christian Yoder (see appendix B). Among the other prisoners confined to the jail were two black men: Jim Haskins, incarcerated for carrying concealed weapons, and Charles Allen, on a charge of burglary. In the presence of such notorious criminals as the Nicely brothers, inevitably, ghoulish stories coupled with the prisoners' superstitions, caused the convicts frantically to implore the sheriff to take them away from the jail on the day of the hanging. They even requested that their hands and feet be bound; anything, to be removed from the jail on the day the Nicely brothers were hanged (*Somerset Herald* 1891, 2 April). Authorities sympathetically complied. Haskins and Allen were removed surreptitiously from the jail and spared from suffering the shadowed aftermath of the hanging.

Murder and hanging ballads are a definite part of American folklore. Considering the ballads that linger long after a murderer's death, there is little doubt that hanging in nineteenth century America captured the minds and imaginations of most people. In the United States, more than anywhere else, a huge number of folk songs and ballads evolved over the years referring to the sorry lives of criminals and their seemingly inevitable end at the gallows. The best-known are those of hero outlaws of the old West, such as Jesse James and Billy the Kid. Most of these ballads, though indulging in a certain amount of hero-worship, nevertheless note that "they got what was coming to them."

Somerset County was no exception. Such a ballad grew from the legend of the Nicely brothers. Copies of the ballad, along with other memorabilia, are still extant. Of the several versions, none claims authorship except one circulated under the name of H. H. Haupt, entitled "The Umberger Murderers." Another version is given the title "The Nicely Brothers Confession." Along with these was Joseph's "Prison Song" (see appendix C). "Prison Song" began to circulate. On occasion, the story of a murderer's execution was related in pamphlet form, usually with heavy moral overtones. Shortly after the brothers were hanged, Edward H. Werner published *The Umberger Tragedy* (Werner 1890, 4-5). The pamphlet was a sincere endeavor, strongly sentimental and melodramatic, but in keeping with similar writings of the day. Oral tradition likewise preserved the Nicely brothers legend, including several variations.

At a conference of the Methodist Episcopal Church in Ligonier on September 8, 1938, a deserving minister who had served Methodist parishes in the Johnstown suburbs of Roxbury and Moxham was, without reservation, elected district superintendent of the Methodist Conference. A standing ovation followed his election signifying a unanimous vote of confidence and support. The tenure of office for the Reverend Emerson Lorenzo Nicely began in the very town where Joseph Nicely was possibly, if not probably, falsely arrested and hung for the murder of Herman Umberger. The Reverend Emerson Lorenzo Nicely was the son of Joseph Nicely.[12]

The Ballad of the Nicely Brothers

We are the Nicely brothers, our names are Joe and Dave
We arrived at Mr. Umberger's by a way that was not paved.
And there attempted robbery and murder followed soon
For which we sit behind the bars to wait upon our doom.

We were taken back to Somerset and placed within the jail
To wait our execution, the time we could not tell.
And when they gave us hearing, it made us both turn pale
To think that we would be taken back to the Somerset County jail.

In court they found us guilty of murder in the first degree
The judge he read the sentence to brother Dave and me.
And when he said that we must hang until we both were dead,
It made the hair rise on their points upon our aching heads.

We were taken back to prison and placed within a cell,
To wait our execution, the time we could not tell.
We sat within our prison and studied night and day
To strike upon some daring plan that we might get away.

By studying until our brains did whirl we struck upon a plan
To attack the deputy sheriff, that daring little man.
We made the break at midday and got out in the hall,
It was there we committed another crime by giving Milt two balls.

We then made tracks to Oak Ridge and thought that we were free;
I hid myself within the brush, Dave climbed upon a tree.
We soon were disappointed, the people came from town,
They found poor Dave upon his perch and demanded he come down.

They made a search all through the ridge, intent on finding me,
They found me hidden within the brush but not upon a tree.
They cheered and yelled and fired off their weapons in the air,
To notify the folks in town that we were in their care.

91

So there we were recaptured, our plan it now had failed;
We were taken back to Somerset and placed within the jail.
Our wives they came to see us and were admitted to our cells,
And how they sobbed and wept while there no tongue can tell.
They said, "Our darling husbands! Oh, you are doomed to die
For the murder of Mr. Umberger which you cannot deny.

When placed within the new jail we made another break,
The rope, it was a failure and proved to be our fate.
With broken bones and aching hearts we tried to make our flight,
I made my way to Barkley's barn and put up for the night.
Poor Dave, he wandered on as far as he could go,
And when he put up for the night it was in Ferner's barn, you know.

So there we laid and suffered beneath the straw and hay,
Till our suffering got so great we could no longer stay.
Poor Dave was first to surrender to William Ferner, you all know
And I to Tony Barkley, who called me from below.
Kind thanks to those two gentlemen who treated us so well-
How often do we thank them within our prison cell.

Come all who have been robbing throughout the Keystone State,
And listen to my story which I will now relate;
For then you will all think it about time for you to quit,
Before behind the prison bars you are compelled to sit.

Our names are Joe and Dave, those names we will never deny,
We leave our loving families in sorrow for to die;
And there's our aged parents, with bent form they do weep,
To think that in a murderer's grave we are compelled to sleep.

Could we undue the crime we did for Umberger's shining till,
We'd cease to roam from friends at home beyond the Laurel Hill.
Oh, had we died when nursing at our dear mother's breast,
Our spirits now would be in heaven aroaming with the blest.

But now we are doomed murderers, our chances are but small,
May God forgive poor Dave and me who through the trap must fall.
Oh, little did we think when in our youthful bloom,
We'd be taken to the scaffold to meet our fateful doom.

92

EPILOGUE

Homecoming

The far-famed Ligonier Valley is one of the most beautiful and fertile regions in the Commonwealth of Pennsylvania. Through it runs the Loyalhanna, a halfway river between the Potomac and the headwaters of the Ohio. It is as renowned for its natural beauty as it is for its significant history. Here, on Sunday afternoon, April 5, 1891, at 2:30 P.M. was enacted the closing chapter in the lives of Joseph and David Nicely. They had been reared, worked, married and raised children in this picturesque valley where their desolate fate would be all but forgotten, only to become legend in neighboring Somerset. The brothers were buried on the knoll of a hill in the family plot on their father's farm.

The obsequies were conducted by Professor W. J. Swigert, a faculty member from Juniata College, Huntington, Pennsylvania.[1] His sermon was based on the text from Psalm 46:1, "God is our refuge and strength, a very present help in trouble." The speaker used a rather striking illustration, typical of the highly emotional sermons of the day, yet not without its poignant message. He was addressing an immense audience, many of whom could not help but wonder what words of wisdom and consolation possibly could be offered considering the tragic circumstances of the occasion. The professor spoke of the time when the great Methodist hymn composer, Charles Wesley, sat before an open window. Hearing a feeble cry of distress, he looked out to see a small bird limping around. Finding no secure refuge, the bird darted through the window and into the refuge of the great man's chest. Moved by the circumstances, Wesley gave to the world the popular and inspiring hymn:

> Jesus lover of my soul
> Let me to thy bosom fly.
> (*Greensburg Daily Tribune* 1891, 7 April)

In his address, before an estimated 800 mourners, Dr. Swigert remarked that their church opposed the death penalty and it was his belief that the state asked too much when it took the lives of the brothers, even if they were guilty. He professed the belief that there was some doubt of the Nicelys' guilt (*Greensburg Daily Tribune* 1891, 7 April). He further stated that the time would come in the lives of those present when what then seemed dark and mysterious would be made plain, and the guilt or innocence of the brothers would be known beyond a shadow of a doubt.

At the request of the families, initially the bodies were not exposed to public view. The decision was reversed, however, as so many attending mourners wished to see the remains of the brothers. The coffins were then placed in two wagons and taken to the family cemetery on the western end of the farm. Upon the arrival of the funeral cortege, and before the coffins were lowered into the graves, the handles were removed and given to the families. David's wife was not present. Some days before the hangings she had, in her own words, said "good-bye to the people of Ligonier forever." Taking her two children with her, she journeyed to Ohio to make her home with relatives.

The *Somerset Herald* reported that on the day the Nicely brothers were hanged, the newspaper published an "extra," devoted entirely to matters and incidents pertaining to the brothers from the time of the murder of Herman Umberger to their arrest, trial and execution. The first edition of 1,500 copies was sold as rapidly as the paper could be taken from the press. One half hour later, a second edition was printed and 5,500 copies struck. Orders were received through the mail for several thousand copies which could not be supplied. The April 8 issue exceeded 8,000 copies (*Somerset Herald* 1891, 8 April).[2]

A series of odd events, occurring both before and after the

deaths of the Nicely brothers, became part of the affair. On the fifth day of the court trial, an advertisement of an unusual but timely nature appeared in the *Somerset Herald* for June 4, 1889. It read:

> In murder trials it is most important to know the exact time at which the crime occurred. To the unfortunate criminal time may be life. In all cases time is money and money can be saved by buying time pieces at Neff and Caseberr's who carry a large assortment; the finest grades of Watches and Clocks, Jewelry and Silverware, Eyeglasses and Spectacles.

The gathering crowd around the courthouse the day of the execution afforded a lucrative field for the operation of pickpockets. At least four victims were accounted for, with an aggregate loss of some five hundred dollars (*Somerset Herald* 1891, 3 April).

In Search of an Alibi

Counsel for the Nicelys proved to be extraordinarily consistent in their belief in the innocence of their clients. They continued to hold the firm opinion that the brothers were victims of false accusations and wrongly condemned for the murder. One of the problems they had faced was that in order to prove their clients guiltless, it was necessary to find the actual criminals. None were found. Yet the attorneys continued to "grasp at straws."

A short time before the murder of Herman Umberger, a traveling phrenologist had been doing a good business in the community. A Mrs. Beale entertained him for several days. Two days before the Umberger murder, she reported a stranger called at her house and asked to see the phrenologist. They both were ushered into the parlor. When Mrs. Beale returned to the room again, she found the two men speaking in hushed whispers. Shortly afterwards, the stranger left. The phrenologist left the next day only to return to the community the Friday after the murder. He was not seen in the community again.

Around 8:00 A.M. the second morning after the murder, a man descended from the mountainside at New Florence, apparently coming from Jennerstown. As he was later described, his clothing and general demeanor strongly resembled that of the Small Man. His appearance was not so much a matter of consideration as the news he brought. He stopped to speak to James Hare and his companions, who were piling railroad ties. The stranger asked if they knew Herman Umberger had been murdered. Hare, who knew the Umbergers, was greatly concerned and requested particulars. The man went on to say that the people of Jennerstown did not know how to conduct an inquest and he was on his way to Johnstown to secure the needed assistance. He then went down to the railroad, and instead of waiting for a passenger train, which was due in a few minutes, he jumped on a freight train.

Following the inquest, it was discovered that the New Florence stranger was in no way connected with the Nicely-Umberger affair. Nor was there any clue about the phrenologist, or the stranger he met with in the home of Mrs. Beale (*Somerset Herald* 1891, 3 April). The defense counsel, hoping to find some lead from these occurrences, were even more concerned when the supposed confession of John Beach appeared. It was discovered by E. P. King, Justice of the Peace in Middlecreek township. Justice King was resting on the front porch of his home, Sunday evening, June 8, 1890, when a stranger walked in and wanted to make a statement. The squire told him that Sunday was not a day for business, but that he could stay the night and take the oath in the morning. The man handed King a document and asked him if he would keep it. The justice took the paper and the man walked away, never to return. Several days later the squire examined it and when he discovered what it was, he forwarded it to the counsel for the Nicely brothers. The confession was badly written and the spelling poor, yet the defense attorneys desperately hoped to establish its validity.

In the confession, Beach stated that he had been in the West and started East in the fall of 1879, accompanied by four other men. They all were from Westmoreland County and were acquainted with one another. When they got to Kansas City, Beach stole a boat to go down the river as far as Missouri. Leaving two of his companions, William Burkholder and Amos Sipe, Beach was caught with the boat and imprisoned for ninety days. Not wanting to be incarcerated under the name of Beach for fear it would be in the newspapers, he adopted another name. Freed, he found his way to Cincinnati and then to Pittsburgh and finally stopped in

Johnstown, where he found work. By this time he had given up his search for Burkholder and Sipe. After some months he became acquainted with a John Miller. Later he returned to Michigan accompanied by Miller. Sometime in their travels they met an acquaintance of Miller's, a book agent. Here the confession became quite vague, as Beach related how the man said he "was looking out for something," and "had some good ones spotted in Somerset County." He gave the names of several farmers, including Benard and Miller, near Garrett; Umberger, near Jennerstown; and others (*Somerset Herald* 1891, 3 April).

Beach's confession claimed that he, Miller, and the book agent had agreed on a place to meet, and there decided on the Umbergers. Beach and Miller were the two at the Umbergers while the book agent and his men stayed outside. He related that a struggle ensued when the pocketbooks with the money were taken. Miller shot three or four times. When he and Miller escaped from the house, they met up with the book agent and his men, and the group headed in the direction of Latrobe. Somewhere, at a fork in the road, they divided the money and threw one of the pocketbooks away. Beach and Miller kept the other, but later dropped it in a small stream. Beach and Miller took one road, and the others took another way. Both Beach and Miller went west again. Before they left, Beach learned that the Nicely brothers had been arrested. In Miller's last letter to Beach, he stated that the Nicelys were still in jail, and that he was returning to Johnstown to go into business. Then came the Johnstown flood and Beach had no more letters from Miller. He believed Miller to have been lost in the flood (*Somerset Herald* 1891, 3 April).

On a train bound for Greensburg, Beach heard a stranger say, "The lady in black is the mother of the Nicely boys." Beach thought that the woman in black had the saddest eyes he had ever seen. He could never forget those eyes. Beach's confession closed by saying that he had delayed making a confession for as long as possible, and by declaring the two boys innocent. He also noted that if Burkholder and Sipe could be found, they would confirm Beach's intention of coming East (*Somerset Herald* 1891, 3 April).

William Burkholder, Amos Sipe and James P. Mountain, three of the men who had been with Beach on the western trip, were found and corroborated the confession—so far as the details of the trip west were concerned. Burkholder had a photograph of Beach taken some years earlier, and King recognized it as bearing a remarkable resemblance to the man he had questioned on that Sunday evening in June. Beach was a tall man, with thick whiskers and a beard heavily tinged with gray. Mountain, in his statement, said he had been approached by a well-dressed stranger and warned that if he gave any testimony in the matter favorable to the Nicelys, he would become unpopular, but that he would be well-rewarded for following instructions (*Somerset Herald* 1891, 3 April).

The John Beach confession resulted in little if any effect on the Nicely case. The Commonwealth's attorneys viewed it as unimportant, and argued that it had been prepared for the purpose of casting doubt in the minds of the members of the pardon board. If the assessment of the prosecuting attorneys was correct, the question remains as to why Beach wanted the brothers to be declared innocent. Interestingly, the reference to Elizabeth Nicely being seen on the train to Greensburg is not without its grain of truth. She had filed conspiracy charges against Constable John O. Rauch and, together with her husband, made frequent trips to the Westmoreland County seat.

Other spurious letters had been written, among them, one written to the "Sheriff of Somerset," and signed simply "Peddler." The letter claimed that the Nicely brothers were innocent, and that he and another peddler (by the name of Fitzsimmons) were guilty of the crime (*Greensburg Daily Tribune* 1891, 1 April).

Finally, there was the following letter, written by one of the jurors:[3]

General W. H. Koontz:

Dear Sir—I drop you a few lines as regards the Nicely case. I have been thinking a great deal about it and am not satisfied. It has been bearing on my mind ever since, it was not my will that it was decided that way. I was sick and hurt, the evidence was not sufficient to convince me of their guilt, and I would have stayed in that juryroom until now if I had not been overpowered by men and sickness.

Will you favor me by going to the Nicelys and telling them I do not want them to have hard feelings toward me, that I tried to do my duty and I could not. Now, Mr. Koontz, let me know what they say. I can see those men's faces before me every night, and I do not like that. Please answer soon.

J. W. Beck (*Somerset Herald*, 1891, 1 April)

Another witness testified that Constable Rauch had confessed to him that he had "doctored" the evidence on which the Nicely brothers were convicted (*Somerset Herald* 1891, 2 April). With the dismissal of both of these testimonies died all hope of acquittal.

Prior to the conviction of Joseph and David, Anthony and his wife Elizabeth had lived in comfortable circumstances.[4] At one time they had donated land for the building of a Brethren Church on their farm (*Somerset Herald* 1891, 3 April). Highly esteemed within their community, Anthony and Elizabeth enjoyed reasonable contentment with family and friends. They owned their home and had savings in a Ligonier bank. Some believed Anthony Nicely to be one of the wealthiest farmers in the Ligonier Valley. But Anthony impoverished himself in the defense of his sons. His resources were completely depleted. Having spent all his funds, judgments for several thousand dollars were entered against him.

Anthony Nicely contended that his sons should never have been tried in Somerset County where major public opinion believed them to be guilty and where the jury was intimidated. Both he and his wife had testified in court that Joseph had dinner with them the night of the murder. Neither mentioned David. Anthony contended that the pocketbook brought into court was not the one sent to his wife, the hat had no hole in it when it was taken away, and the handkerchief and overalls were the same style and pattern worn by numerous other men (*Somerset Herald* 1891, 3 April).

In summing up his impressions, General Alexander H. Coffroth believed that seldom in criminal history had there been a concurrence of so many adverse circumstances and at a time when each one of them proved fatal to the arguments the defense had projected. Just the week before their counsel went to the Supreme Court, Joseph and David broke out of jail and Joseph shot the deputy sheriff. As a result, the newspapers characterized the brothers as dangerous desperadoes intent on murder. As their attorneys were about to appear before the pardon board, the brothers made their second escape. This, Coffroth believed, became magnified and distorted as it become known to the members of the board. While meeting with Governor Beaver, saws were found in the Nicely brothers' cells. Finally, there was the strange affair of Dr. Orth wrongly diagnosing Joseph insane.[5] Circumstance and mounting adverse opinion had condemned the brothers from the beginning.

The Umberger home passed into the hands of strangers. After the tragedy, Mrs. Umberger and her grandchildren went to live with her son-in-law, Reuben Horner. Ella Stern was employed by another family who lived several miles from Jennerstown. For a while the farm was rented by a man named Humbert from Berlin. He did not remain long. Inevitably, the house was claimed to be haunted. Fireside legend holds that when dusk begins to fall, familiar objects become indistinct and assume fantastic forms. The old alarm bell that summoned neighbors on the night Herman Umberger was murdered tolls dismally two or three times. Then three shadowy forms come from the back door leading out from the kitchen. First to appear are two men, one tall and one short, both with their faces concealed. In hot pursuit follows the gaunt form of old farmer Umberger "with the pallor of death upon his face and blood flowing from his breast." The two men press on, closely followed by the ghost of the old farmer. They glide over the soft plowed land without leaving a track, melting through fences like a mist. Over the fields and down the hollow, pursued and pursuer continue until they are lost in the woods (*Somerset Herald* 1891, 8 April).

This ghost story depleted the value of the Umberger farm. It contained 135 acres of some of the best land in Somerset County, with large and substantial farm buildings. The home also lost its value. As time passed by, few signs of the tragedy remained. Yet, for quite a while the bullet holes remained in the walls, evidence that the assassin three times missed his victim. The old bell, with its rope coming through the ceiling into the kitchen, had been removed. The property no longer was referred to as the Umberger farm. With the coming of a more realistic age, even the ghosts became only a memory.

One cannot help being both baffled and fascinated by the personality of Joseph Nicely. Certainly he was elusive and enigmatic, riding with Jesse James as a young man, wanted for arson in Ohio and, if not the murderer of Herman Umberger, at least a member of the gang responsible for his death. On the other hand, he certainly was not feared by everyone. He was remembered as a handsome man, and a devoted father and husband. And there are numerous references to the quality of his high tenor voice, which was often heard in a local church choir.

Joseph possessed a sizable library, which he willed to be divided among his seven children. After his second escape, he stated to a newspaper reporter, "I am sorry that our plans failed. If I had gotten to the Laurel Hill they would not get me. I know every foot of that mountain and not less than twenty caves, some of them not as large as a man's body at the mouth, but as large as this cell inside. It's hard to suffer for another man's crime and any man who stops to think would not blame us for attempting to save our lives" (*Somerset Herald* 1891, 3 April). Could these be the words of a "dangerous desperado intent on murder?"

The day before the brothers were hanged, David made his confession. Joseph made no public confession. One has to ask whether there was any need for Joseph to make a confession. Again, when interviewed by a reporter from the *Somerset Herald*, Joseph declared, as he did in his diary, that "we" were innocent. Here he used the inclusive "we." He upheld David's contention that though present, David was not the murderer. Joseph added that he was not near the Umberger home the day of the murder. He was reminded that the Vannears had testified to seeing him with David going up the Laurel Mountain toward Jennerstown. Joseph denied the charge, adding that he and the Vannears had not been on friendly terms. He had rented a shop from Vannear in Ligonier. There had been a dispute over rent and Vannear had sued him. "I won the case," said Joseph, and Vannear told Joseph, "he would make him pay for it." "I have always had money. I owned a little farm and worked for my father and the neighbors. I never was without a few dollars and owed no one. I was happy and contented and coveted no one's wealth" (*Somerset Herald* 1891, 1 April).

In substance, David stated that he was present when Herman Umberger was killed, but that he did not murder him. When he left his home on February 27, 1889, it was for robbery, but not for murder. He only learned that it was Umberger who was to be robbed when well on the way. In this confession David makes no reference to Joseph. Nor does he say who accompanied him to the Umberger home. These words strongly imply "orders" from somewhere, which may explain why General Alexander H. Coffroth wanted the brothers tried separately. There are those in the Ligonier Valley who, throughout the next century, secretly believed that Joseph Nicely was not the murderer of Herman Umberger.

Joseph's diary, his last letter to his wife, and the last letter he received from his wife are most revealing and give a new perspective to his position in the macabre affair. After Joseph's death, the diary and the two letters supposedly fell into the hands of Sheriff Milton McMillan. Neither the diary nor the letters surfaced again until 1988, when they were given to the Somerset County Historical Museum.[6] In reviewing the diary and letters, one finds it difficult to believe that they contain the thoughts of the man who murdered Herman Umberger. Written with small crammed letters and numerous misspelled words and sentences running together, the diary evidences sincerity and strong emotional feelings on the part of the writer. Whatever his reasons may have been for keeping the diary, Joseph puts into words his innermost thoughts, obviously not to color his public image, but as a record of his own private thoughts. In his last letter to his wife, he wrote that he wanted her to have the diary as "it will be of value to you." Harriet Nicely never received her husband's diary.

Covering the period September 16, 1889, to March 18, 1890, recurring refrains in the diary are references to "my dear wife," the horrible food, the bitter cold, and the loneliness of the prison cell. The diary includes numerous tirades against the officials of the jail, attorneys for the Commonwealth, the local newspapers, and witnesses and officers who falsely testified for the prosecution. Joseph likewise struck out at presiding Judge Baer whom he believed, along with the jury, to have been intimidated. The "Albright preacher," as Joseph referred to him, also comes in for a few choice expletives. Joseph remonstrates the minister for the part he played in Joseph's recapture at the time of the first prison escape. The minister had been in hot pursuit of the brothers, and as they were disappearing in the woods, fired shots after them. One bullet seared Joseph's hair. Joseph found it hard to believe that such actions were those of a minister of the Gospel.

The diary records repeated references to Deputy Sheriff

McMillan. Joseph claimed he had been carried away in the excitement of the moment, and did not mean to shoot McMillan— but only to frighten him, at the time the brothers attempted their first escape. At first, when it was reported that the deputy sheriff was dying, Joseph wrote that he could not eat nor sleep and became quite ill thinking about it (Joseph Nicely 1889, diary 16 September).[11] My prayer is that he will get well" (Diary 1889, 18 September). During the days that followed, leading to McMillan's progressive recovery, there are frequent references to his welfare. "Milt is getting better as fast as possible. People make it worse to me than it really is." A repeated notation in the diary is "Milt is getting better! Milt is getting better!" (Diary 1889, 23 September) On October 1 he records, "Milt was in to see me today. He is going about now." Within hours of Joseph being hanged, there was an emotional parting between Joseph and Deputy Sheriff McMillan when Joseph asked for the Deputy Sheriff's forgiveness (*Somerset Herald* 1891, 8 April).

A surprising notation in the diary is Joseph's statement that it was David who insisted upon breaking jail and making their first escape. In most respects, Joseph was the spokesman and the decision maker for the two brothers but in this instance, Joseph claimed that David was the instigator. "David would not give me no (sic) rest day or night. At last I consented although very reluctantly (Joseph Nicely 1889, diary 17 September).

His venom against Judge Baer continued. "There is a ring here who runs things to suit themselves. Judge Baer was intimidated by this ring. This ring would do anything to hang us no matter how innocent we may prove ourselves to be. They would not believe any person from Westmoreland County who would swear in our behalf" (Diary 1889, 17 September).

"I am always dreaming of home," Joseph records on September 27. On the same day he told of being chained to his cell as the guards had become alerted to rumors that assistance in one way or another was arriving to bring about the brothers' freedom (Diary 1889, 27 September). "I am cold and I am chained. I must go to bed to keep warm. Coffroth sent me four novels yesterday. I would sooner if they had been Bibles" (Diary 1889, 24 September). He writes of feeling dirty and miserable with no change of clothing for over five weeks. (Diary 1889, 3 October) "I had a headache nearly all last night and troubled dreams." "I do not feel good this morning but I trust in God . . . I pray eight or ten times each day for God is with me" (Diary 1889, 14 October). With the anxiety that is building up within him, he lashes out again against the community and the minister who tried to murder him. "God will certainly visit this town as he did Sodom and Ghomora (sic) in the days of old for the righteous is scarce here. I think there might be a few but I have not seen them yet because you know a tree by the fruit it bears. Why did the Evangelical preacher of this place try to murder me?" (Diary 1889, 18 October)

"I cannot collect thoughts to think the Supreme Court has refused us a new trial" (Diary 1889, 16 November). As the diary continues Joseph makes many references to prayer. His complaints about the food are never ending but he commends the sheriff with slight praise for his Christmas rations (Diary 1889, 25 December). "We have been getting nothing more than bread and water." He [the sheriff] came in this morning and said he did not blame Dave or me for anything as he never heard us say a word" (Diary 1890, 5 January). Evidently, for one reason or another, Joseph's venom was found only in his diary, not in formal complaints.

On January 25, Joseph wrote a poem which he entitled "Prison Song." In his own unpolished way, his feelings of an unrecognized innocence are not unlike Oscar Wilde's "De Profundis." The poem is a plea that comes "out of the depths" of his being. He writes of happy times and places of his childhood. He laments the circumstances that placed the brothers in the Somerset jail. He holds to the belief that he and David will yet go free. One of Joseph's most interesting notations is for February 6. He writes, "if EG would have done what I wanted done I would be safe now but he never done what I wanted him to do from the first time he came here"[7] (Joseph Nicely 1890, diary 6 February). Later, he makes reference to a letter from his wife which the sheriff carried in his pocket for a week (Diary 1890, 9 February). "A great many people came to see us today and the majority are in sympathy with us" (Diary 1890, 24 February). Notations of the bad food, troubled dreams, depressing snows and the cold are repeated references until March 18 when the diary ends. "Tuesday morning clear and snow melting. Pardon Board gives us another month yet, until April 15" (Diary 1890, 18 March).

Joseph's last letter to his wife was written the day he was hanged. He expressed his thoughts concerning religious matters and how he desired his possessions to be divided among his children. The division of his books evidences a sizeable library and that Joseph himself devoted much time to reading. A letter dated November 23, 1890 from his wife, Harriet, also was found with his prison diary. She writes of her discouragement but "still I think there will be something turn up to show the fraud that has been in this case for certainly unjust care cannot stand." She continues with an account of the school attendance of the children and reference is made to the sale of corn from the fall harvest. She is keeping the family farm in working order with the help of the older children. "I am still hoping that something will show up yet to show that your are innocent." Significantly, these private letters were not intended as confessions or for public viewing. Accidently surfacing a century after the conviction, both Harriet's letter and Joseph's letter to her attest to a strong bond between them, which also was found in the many references Joseph makes to his wife in his diary. These letters evidence a strong spiritual nature in both husband and wife. Of note is Joseph's concern for the religious education of his children, and Harriet's belief in her husband's innocence.

David, however, is mostly portrayed as a silent participant, both the night of the murder and throughout his prison sentence. Despite his presence and involvement at the Umberger home, his role is that of an indifferent accomplice caught in the affair, but somehow distant from it and an enigma to it. Other than his insistence, according to Joseph's diary, on their first attempted escape from the Somerset jail, David was the one who remained in the shadows and took orders rather than gave them. He is almost pathetic in his naivete. His confession rings with a definiteness that is resolute with his belief in his own innocence. He viewed himself as a participant in robbery but as an involuntary victim in murder. Destined to do what he was instructed to do in the Umberger parlor, he played the role, not only of the "tall man," but the "other man." Firing his pistol into the ceiling, for no other reason but to frighten, he viewed himself neither as an accomplice nor a participant, though his very presence would completely discredit his claim. In no way excusing himself from his share in robbery, he confessed he did not make the trip to Somerset County for murder. He did not know that he and his companion in crime were going to the Umberger home until they were on their way. Orders. The man of mystery, whoever the true murderer might be, was the man who dispersed the bullets into the body of Herman Umberger.

Despite the fascination the case of the Nicely brothers holds after more than a century, there still remains unresolved questions that would raise more than reasonable doubt as to their guilt. Why did Joseph and David, with their seemingly comfortable backgrounds, each having property given to them by their father, and families of their own, choose to be part of a gang of robbers, engaging in the pursuits of common outlaws? Would the allure of the James brothers, and the brothers' relationship with them have anything to do with their small town robberies? Joseph spent a summer riding with the James gang. David named one of his sons Jesse. Why, at the final moment, was David's life shrouded with further mystery when his wife, with their two children, deserted him? Why did he not mention Joseph in his confession, if not for the protection of another party? Had the clothing worn by the suspects on the night of the murder been "doctored" by John O. Rauch, as claimed by a witness, giving reason to Elizabeth Nicely to bring charges against him for conspiracy? Had the brothers been given separate court trials, would there have been a different verdict? Due to the emotional and psychological climate of the day, brought about by other robberies and murders, and the need for suspects to be located quickly—and with only circumstantial evidence—was Joseph Nicely wrongly accused? Lastly, and most poignant of all, is the question of Herman Umberger himself.

Judge Robert Ralston, in his book *Delay in the Execution of Murderers*, raises the question as to whether there could have been more behind the murder of Herman Umberger than what took place February 27, 1889 (Ralston 1911, R3-82).[8] Judge Ralston contends that Herman Umberger was a co-conspirator rather than a victim. Unfortunately, in his records, he does not explain his reason for making this statement. He does, however, leave behind a legacy of unchallenged integrity in jurisprudence. What were his reasons for recording the statement? Could the reason for the murder have been more than robbery, a connection between the murderer and Herman Umberger? If the two letters accompanying the diary of

Joseph Nicely and the supposition of Judge Ralston be considered together, it would appear that the true murderer of Herman Umberger, was not Joseph Nicely but someone whom the brothers could not, dare not disclose. The man who held the key to unlock these unanswered mysteries was and remains, unknown. There are those among the living who believe they know who holds that key. Only time will answer the question. Who killed Herman Umberger?

Conclusion

More than a century after Samuel de Champlain had founded Quebec, and had established Port Royal as a fur trading post, the coureurs de bois or woodrangers had floated their canoes down the St. Lawrence, across the Great Lakes to the Rocky Mountains. A few hunters, in like spirit, from the province of William Penn's Western Woods, stood at the foot of the Allegheny Mountains weighing the hazards of a season in an uncharted wilderness (Doyle 1945, 16). Drawn as much by the mystery of the virgin hinterlands as for the profits they made in fur trading, they were young men with a taste for solitary adventure and a readiness to adapt to the Indian's way of life. By the middle of the 1700s, a few adventuresome fur traders and scouts had wandered into southwestern Pennsylvania, having dared to scale the Indian's Endless Mountains. The land was still unexplored by colonial settlers. The white explorers were quick to discover why the Iroquois made claims so far south of their settlements in New York state. Here dense forests provided a natural haven for deer and other animals, providing excellent hunting in the woodlands and fishing in the mountain streams. Old Indian trails crossed the mountains. The two Indian trails which were considered most reliable were the Northern route and Nemacolin's trail.

Although Penn's grant from the British crown called for most of this land, Penn realized that the Indians had some rights in the territory and obtained from them cessions of land included in his grant from the crown. By the Treaty of Fort Stanwix in November 5, 1768, the Indians relinquished their rights to the vast area of land embracing what is now Somerset County (*Early Somerset County History*, 3). All the forbidden lands were purchased from the Indians for the sum of ten thousand dollars. "Just who the first person to receive the first warrant in what is now Somerset County will never be known" (Doyle 1945, 37).

The shortest distance between the Atlantic settlements and the Ohio valley was by way of these two Indian trails, both of which crossed the territory. Notable among the land speculators was the Ohio Company that had been granted 400,000 acres of land along the Ohio (Doyle 1945, 18). Christopher Gist, a surveyor from North Carolina, was appointed to search out and discover these lands. For his first journey Gist chose the southern route, the Nemacolin Trail. He was the first white man known to have crossed what is now Somerset County. Having blazed a white man's trail across the mountain barriers, Gist set out the following year to search out a more northern route. On Monday, November 5, 1750, Gist and his party reached the top of the Allegheny Mountains, traveling over the old Northern Indian Trail. Gist left a very complete journal from which we learn the places where he and his party stopped and the distances between them. In 1752, Gist built a cabin and induced eleven families to settle with him (Cassady 1932, 82).

Early settlers from a variety of European backgrounds, brought with them a diversity of customs and skills. They were overwhelmingly English, though there were some Dutch, Swedish, Scottish, Welsh and Irish. Added to this was a flow of French Huguenots and German immigrants. German manual dexterity and mechanical inventiveness, together with German agricultural methods, made the Pennsylvania Germans among the most prosperous and progressive of settlers in the English colonies. They not only engaged in printing, as did Somerset's own immigrant Frederich Goeb, but also papermaking and glassblowing. Their canvass-topped Conestoga wagons led the westward movement.

Pennsylvania was one of the principal channels of that movement. Philadelphia had been, and continues to be, a leading port of entry. Braddock and Forbes had cut primitive military roads into the southwestern part of the state and Pennsylvanians had created the first trans-Allegheny frontier. Pittsburgh was the Gateway to the West when white civilization terminated in the Ohio Valley, and in later years the Pennsylvania or the State Road, and the National Road that followed the Nemacolin Trail, had carried a flood of settlers into that western territory.

Steeped in legend, artifacts forge an indelible link with the past.

Each has a tale to tell, whether in epic chapter or footnote. Such artifacts open a window on the past, helping us to understand our heritage. Somerset's artifacts are well-preserved and beautifully displayed in the Somerset County Historical and Genealogical Society Museum. Numerous markers along Route 30 are reminders of important landmarks associated with the Old Forbes Military Road. Libraries house historical records. The Somerset County jail holds a display case exhibiting articles of clothing and other memorabilia connected with the Nicely brothers murder trial. All are a part of the mountain saga spun from a remembered past by the Frosty Sons of Thunder.[9] It all began on what was once a buffalo trail and became the famous Pennsylvania Turnpike, the first superhighway of its kind in the nation.

The story of the Pennsylvania Turnpike is fascinating. A section of it passes through the northern part of Somerset County. An important development in world highway history occurred in Pennsylvania on May 21, 1937, when Governor George H. Earle signed an act creating the Pennsylvania Turnpike Commission who then built the first modern four-lane turnpike in the United States (Shank 1988, 61). It closely parallels the Lincoln Highway, which was earlier known as the Pennsylvania Road, and as the John Forbes Military Road. The story of the first superhighway of its kind may be told in many ways. It can be described with vital statistics, such as construction costs, tonnages, receipts and expenditures, all of which are important to an understanding of the project. From another perspective, from the Laurel Ridge to the Allegheny Mountains, the hills and valleys echo past legends remembered for their pioneer romance and colonial mystique. An automobile trip between these two mountains along the Pennsylvania Turnpike is an excursion into hills and valleys that were once so hidden from the sun that early pioneers referred to them as the Shades of Death. The Laurel Hill contains ancient caves that once housed in their small caverns the counterfeit money of David "Robber" Lewis and served as hiding places for Joseph and David Nicely. Through this section of the country roamed the lone Mountain Jack as a helping friend to the troubled traveler and dreaded foe of the Indian. Colonial affairs brought George Washington back to the county no less than eleven times (Doyle 1945, 20). The iron will of General John Forbes built a military road that became the main artery between east and west. His secret romantic dream was revealed to his officers on the top of the Allegheny Mountains. The first Bible to be printed west of the Alleghenies was printed in Somerset in 1813 by Frederick Goeb. These well-known historical personalities and others, have left their mark in the land between the mountains. Often with the speed and ease we travel the Pennsylvania Turnpike, we are apt to forget the trials of pioneers and early settlers in scaling the mountains over crude and underdeveloped roads in a seemingly endless battle to overcome natural obstacles. The Pennsylvania Turnpike was a dream that could not be realized until the twentieth century.

Throughout the nineteenth century, the conquest of America's wide-open spaces was no less important than the conquest of the Indian to the development of this land by the white man. When the Constitution was launched in 1789, primitive methods of travel were still in use. Early settlers found travel to be one of the most difficult of problems because of the dense forests, many swamps and the rough terrain encountered through much of the Somerset region (Baldwin 1964, 15). The Forbes Military Road, which crossed this area from east to west, became the first important route for packhorse trains traveling between Philadelphia and Pittsburgh. Packhorse trains continued to carry the few products of the settlers, mostly furs, hides and whiskey over the mountain to eastern markets. These were traded for articles like knives, salt, flour, utensils and tools. The trip required almost a month depending upon weather conditions. In time small improvements were made and Forbes Military Road became known as the Great Road or the Pennsylvania Road. A short time before 1800, the covered or Conestoga wagon completely replaced the packhorse train (Baldwin, 78). Followed shortly thereafter by stage coaches, the wagons crept over abominable roads and travel still remained a most formidable task.

The skills required for building durable roads had been developed in Britain and France and the earliest American examples, similar to good European highways, were built along the eastern states. The earliest solution to the problem of hauling passengers and freight over land was the hard-surfaced road, after the principle of the Scottish engineer, John Louden McAdam. In 1794, Pennsylvania led in the progression of a road system with a privately built road from Philadelphia to Lancaster called a turnpike or pike, because at the toll houses the road was barred by a pole (pike) that was swung aside after the toil was paid. The financial success of the Lancaster Pike led to the chartering of hundreds of other toll-road turnpikes (Baldwin 1969, 231). Completed in 1795, it was the first scientifically designed road in the United States (Shank 1988, 35–36).

Without a doubt the most dramatic changes in the pre-Civil War years was the shift in the direction of the nation's internal commerce. The Pennsylvania Road and rougher trails such as the Wilderness Trail into Kentucky were barely adequate for the movement of settlers. They did not begin to answer the West's need for cheap and efficient transportation. Turnpikes did make it possible to transport goods across the Allegheny Mountains, but the expense made it almost prohibitive. Until the coming of the railroad, cheap land transportation over great land distances was impossible. Ultimately, the canals could not handle the huge exports of the growing West, and an entirely new means of transportation emerged with the railroad. The 1840s dealt a death blow to both the turnpikes and the canals.

The feverish years after the Civil War witnessed an unparalleled outburst of railroad construction. Not to be outdone was William H. Vanderbilt who envisioned a new railroad between Harrisburg and Pittsburgh, known as the South Pennsylvania Railroad (Walton 1982, 2-4). The roadbed would parallel, with slight variations, the Pennsylvania Road. When Vanderbilt sent his expert engineers to explore the mountains and valleys of the Alleghenies in 1881, Pittsburgh already was being served by two railroad systems, both originating on the Atlantic coastal plain. The Pennsylvania Railroad followed the Susquehanna Valley beyond Harrisburg and into the valleys of the Juniata and the Conemaugh. The Baltimore and Ohio railroad paralleled the Potomac and Youghiogheny Rivers. Yet Vanderbilt went ahead with his project and completed the construction of nine tunnels through the seven mountains of southwestern Pennsylvania (Walton 1982, 23–33). The railroad was never completed. Competition changed Vanderbilt's venture into "Vanderbilt's Folly." On September 12, 1885, according to Alvin F. Harlow in his *The Road of the Century* ,"work ceased forever on the South Pennsylvania Railroad" (Walton 1982, 39). Though

Vanderbilt's attempt ended in failure, his men left behind the physical evidence of an incomplete road bed and nine tunnels (Walton, 23-33).

Six attempts were made between 1886 and 1938 to rejuvenate the South Pennsylvania Railroad before its right-of-way was purchased by the Pennsylvania Turnpike Commission (Walton 1982, 40). The last attempt to use the South Pennsylvania Railroad's right-of-way and tunnels between Pittsburgh and Harrisburg was recorded in *The Traffic World* magazine of June 11, 1938. Application was made to the Commission in Finance of the Interstate Commerce Commission for a "Pittsburgh Harrisburg Short Line" "to construct and operate a high-speed diesel-electric passenger and freight railroad between Pittsburgh and Harrisburg making use of the right-of-way and tunnels of the South Pennsylvania Railroad. However, it remained only a proposal. A bill was passed by the 1937 General Assembly of the Commonwealth of Pennsylvania creating the Pennsylvania Turnpike Commission, for the purpose of constructing, operating, maintaining and financing a superhighway between Harrisburg and Pittsburgh along the former route of the South Pennsylvania Railroad. The first contract for construction of the turnpike was let on October 26, 1938, and the contractor began work the next day (Walton 1982, 42-43; cf. *The Traffic World* 1938, 11 June).

The story of the demise of the South Pennsylvania Railroad would not be complete without mentioning that a small portion of the South Pennsylvania Railroad roadbed, less than five miles, was used by the Pittsburgh, Westmoreland and Somerset Railroad that operated between Ligonier and Somerset for a brief time. This involved the use of the Quemahoning Tunnel—the only tunnel on the South Pennsylvania that was finished and used before the Pennsylvania Turnpike Commission took over the South Pennsylvania right-of-way. The Pittsburgh, Westmoreland and Somerset Railroad was begun on June 14, 1899 (Walton 1982, 43–45).

On May 26, 1906, the train, with several log cars and two passenger coaches on the rear, steamed out of Ligonier at 10:25 A.M., scheduled to arrive at Somerset at 12:00 noon. There were thirteen stops between Ligonier and Somerset. The Pittsburgh, Westmoreland and Somerset Railroad was popular in its day, remembered for its pleasant excursions and colorful mountain lumbermen and railroad operators, but its tenure was short-lived (Walton 1982, 43-45). Among other reasons for its demise was a gradual decrease in freight and passenger earnings. Equipment was in disrepair. The railroad was no longer the convenience it once had been. The railroad's title was bought in 1917 by the Pittsburgh, Cincinnati, Chicago and St. Louis Railroad and the PW&S remained "only a scar on the wooded hills" (Walton 1982, 46).

The Pennsylvania Turnpike was a unique innovation. No one had ever seen a road without traffic lights, intersections, steep hills and sharp curves. As the first all-weather, limited access superhighway, the Pennsylvania Turnpike was to serve as a model for a wave of superhighway construction throughout the country.

Since the opening of the Pennsylvania Turnpike in 1940, travelers have come from every state in the union and many foreign countries. Traveling through the county at an accelerated speed, most have neither the time nor the inclination to stop and consider the legends associated with the Old Forbes Military Road between the Laurel Hill and the Allegheny Mountains nor the impact that the legend of Joseph and David Nicely has upon the Frosty Sons of Thunder to this day.

Long before the advent of the Pennsylvania Turnpike, the Old West or the frontier that was once Somerset was long gone. There still remain some well-preserved covered bridges to remind us of the past. An occasional log cabin, mostly remodeled, is still to be found in out-of-the-way places. A long Pennsylvania rifle may be found treasured in a gun case, or displayed above an old stone fireplace. Markers still designate the remains of redoubts and forts along the Old Forbes Military Road. Historically speaking, Somerset County is still young, even in the new world. At the time Christopher Gist, George Washington, General Edward Braddock and General John Forbes were pondering the problem of opening a road through the tangled wilderness across the Allegheny Mountain and the Laurel Hill to the Ohio Valley, Spanish settlements in America were old, their government buildings, churches, schools and marketplaces were green with the moss of two centuries and their halls were filled with ancient intrigue. "But the broad pattern of a new world was being spun on the wide loom of destiny, and the part of Bedford County, Pennsylvania, which was finally woven into that pattern on April 17, 1795, as Somerset County, was to portray one of the most brilliant of all the colorful designs" (Doyle 1945, 60).

A diary dated June 5, 1771, records a horseman picking his way through the forests along a mountain stream. The horse is foam-flecked from the long, hard climb up the eastern side of the Allegheny mountain. The rider sits erect in his saddle, dodging now and then an overhanging hemlock bough or the leaning trunk of an oak. When he reaches the top of the mountain, the sun is already low over the western rim of the Laurel Hill. The rider watches with some apprehension from under the shade of his broad-brimmed hat. Approaching a natural meadow, he takes mental notes to be later recorded in his journal that he carries in his saddle bag.

This valley is what properly may be termed rolling in general features, divided into hills, bottoms, and glades; generally densely timbered, and with little or no underbrush, the bottoms open and sodded with short fine grass. As to the glades, nothing could exceed in beauty and luxuriance these plains—in many places, for acres, grass as high as man, of a bluish color, with feathery heads of bluish purple.

The man draws his reins. Rising in his stirrups he looks to the west. Wood smoke is spiraling up from the low ridge a short distance ahead. For an instant all the weariness of the day gives way to a feeling of exaltation; for at last, he has found the friend whom he knows to be one of the first settlers on that beautiful land west of the Allegheny Mountains. Harmon Husband, better known as Toscape Death, settles back in his saddle. Resolutely, he urges his horse toward the column of friendly smoke ((Doyle 1945, 9-10).[10] His longtime friend, and the colorful adventures and people awaiting the coming days. Joseph and David Nicely ended the era of history turned legend in Somerset County. Harmon Husband, one of Somerset's earliest pioneers, descending the western slope of the Allegheny Mountains, began what is now the remembered treasures of the Frosty Sons of Thunder.

APPENDIX A

'Mongst the Hills of Somerset

by James Whitcomb Riley

'Mongst the Hills o'Somerset—
Wish I was a'roamin' yet;
My feet won't get used to
These lowlands I'm trampin' through.
Wisht I could go back there, and
Stroke the long grass with my hand,
Like my schoolboy sweetheart's hair,
Smoothed out underneath it there.
Wisht I could set eyes once more
On our shadders, on before,
Climbin' in the airly dawn,
Up the slopes 'at love growed on.
Natcherel as the violet
'Mongst the Hills o'Somerset.

How 't u'd rest a man like me
Just fer 'bout an hour to be
Up there, where the mornin' air
Could reach out and catch me there!—
Snatch my breath away, and then
Rinse and give it back again,
Fresh as dew, and smellin' of
The old pink I us't to love;
And a-flavori'n ev'ry breeze
With mixed hints o'mulberries
And May-apples, from the thick
Bottom lands along the crick
Where the fish bite, dry or wet,
'Mongst the Hills o'Somerset.

Like a livin' pictur', things
All come back; and bluebird sings
In the maple, tongue and bill
Thrillin' glory fit to kill!
In the orchard, jay and bee
Ripin the first pears to me;
And the "Prince's harvest," they
Tumble to me where I lay
In the clover, provin' still
"A boy's will is the wind's will,"
Clean forgot is time, and care
And thick hearin', and gray hair;—
But there's nothin' I forget
'Mongst the Hills o'Somerset.

Middle-aged—to be egzact
Very middle-aged, in fact-
Yet a'thinkin' back to them,
I'm the same wild boy again,
There's the dear old home and more,
And there's mother at the door-
Dead, I know for thirty year,
Yet she's singin'; and I hear;
And there's Joe and Mary Jane;
And Pap, comin' up the lane;
Dusk's a-fallin'; and the dew
'Pears like it's a-fallin too—
Dreamin' we're all livin' yet—
'Mongst the Hills o'Somerset.

"Mongst the Hills of Somerset" was originally printed in the *Century Magazine* in November 1888, and later was published in *Poems Here at Home* in 1893. Although there are Somerset Hills in Indiana, Mr. Riley did not know it when he wrote this poem in Hoosier dialect. The idea was suggested in the office of the *Pittsburgh Bulletin* during the course of a random conversation with the editor, John W. Black, who "alluded to the trout fishing in Somerset County, among other things, and had incidentally used the expression 'mongst the hills o'Somerset' in describing the picturesque nooks of that nearby locality, when Riley was observed suddenly to fidget about in his chair, then to roll his eyes in a state of intense pleasure at something, and finally was heard to break out with the joyful exclamation: 'I'll make a poem about that!' and he did, literally building the poem up, idea and all, within the next few hours, on the basis of one line then suggested. . . . The dialect of the verses doesn't apply to Somerset County at all, being the same old Hosier idiom that Riley had made famous in all his poems; whereas the dialect of the Somerset Mountains is notoriously the most homely Pennsylvania Dutch in Pennsylvania! However, the question of anachronism is of no consequence, for, so far as the poem is concerned, it might apply to any other hills of Somerset that the broad topography of all America may be noted for."

It is interesting to note that Mr. Riley's father and grandparents were born and lived in a portion of the original Bedford County (now Somerset County, Pennsylvania) before they came to Indiana.

The Historical and Genealogical Society of Somerset County has a copy of this version of the poem together with a summary of how the poem came to be written.

APPENDIX B

The McCellandtown Gang

In addition to the Nicely brothers, the Somerset jail contained the infamous McCellandtown Gang, seven men and three women. They were sentenced and convicted to long terms of imprisonment in the penitentiary for robbing and brutally torturing Christian Yoder, a well-known Amish resident of Summit township.

On the evening of April 13, 1889, four masked men entered the home of Yoder, just after the family, consisting of Yoder, his wife, hired girl and hired man, had finished eating their evening meal. Covering the family with revolvers, the men commanded Yoder to turn over all the money he had to them. He gave the robbers $100 but they believed he had more. When he could not produce more money they threatened to burn his barn and hang him. They also demanded he write orders on farmers who were indebted to him. This he refused to do.

The brutal torture and robbery of Christian Yoder further alarmed the county, taking place as closely as it did to the murder of Herman Umberger. A posse was organized to invade the hiding places of the gang, which were known to be in Fayette County. The following graphic account of the capture was given in the May 1, 1889, *Somerset Herald*:

> Charles Lewis, the leader of the gang, was believed to be staying at a place called "Hill House." It was from this house that the gang had made their escape when Fayette county officials attempted their capture. The house was built of logs and weatherboarded, facing the Brandonville road. W. B. Hill, a member of the gang, was the proprietor. Sheriff Kyle, of Myersdale, and his party, had been designated to make another attempt at their capture. They closed in upon the house where W. B. Hill and his wife were found and arrested. Three other men were discovered upstairs. Mrs. Hill pleaded with the

men to surrender as escape appeared impossible. Among the men was Charles Lewis, the celebrated and fearless leader of the gang, who quietly submitted to having a pair of handcuffs placed on his wrists. The others likewise surrendered to their captors.

A final capturing of the prisoners numbered ten, who were taken to Confluence, and then to Meyersdale where a hearing was held. Justice W. B. Cook committed the entire band to the Somerset county jail. The entire McClellandtown gang was given a hearing before Judge Bear. The women were discharged. The trial for the men came up at the regular May term of court; Charles J. Lewis, Decantur Tasker, Jackson Sullivan and Marshall Sullivan were convicted on May 30. The prisoners were sentenced to ten years separate and solitary confinement in the Western Penitentiary (Cf. Werner 1890, II: 1-8).

APPENDIX C

Prison Song

by Joseph Nicely

When my mind wanders back
To my happy childhood days-
The days that are now forever past;
Where my brothers and sisters played
Around the dear old cottage home-
These are the thoughts stamped on my memory to last.

Chorus:

If your heart was ever sad-
Then these thoughts should make you glad,
When you think of the morning you'll be free;
For then you'll cross the prison floor
And go out the prison door,
For there's many happy days you yet may see.

But as the days and months go by
Ah! the years! how swift they fly!
But our future there is no one who can tell;
For this is left within the hands
Of the One that ever stands,
And says- "Trust in me and all things will be well."

Chorus:

In the dark and gloomy cell
There is no one who can tell
How anxiously we wait the news to hear-
That our freedom we have gained

And no longer will be chained,
And the laws of Somerset no longer fear.

Chorus:

Oh the sadness in my heart!
When I think that I must part
From the friend of life who is so dear to me;
That I may never more may be
Roaming o'er this land so free,
As the birds that sing upon the leafy tree.

Chorus:

But these thoughts may not be so
And from prison we may go,
If a trial fair by jury we may see;
Then with friends we can rejoice,
And with one united voice,
Praise the God whose hand did surely set us free.

Chorus.

"Joseph Nicely belonged to the Evangelical Church and the result of the religious training he received is shown by the poem, "Prisoner Song," composed in jail" (*Somerset Herald* 1891, 3 April).

APPENDIX D

The Board of Pardons in the Pennsylvania Department of Justice kept a record of the numerous petitions and letters proclaiming the innocence of the Nicely brothers. Below is a photocopy of the beginning of one of the legal petitions to the Board of Pardons made by the Nicelys' attorneys. According to John A. Nicely, great grandson of Joseph Nicely, who searched the Board of Pardon's microfilm records, the approximate number of signatures of citizens from both Somerset and Ligonier on the petitions runs close to two thousand.

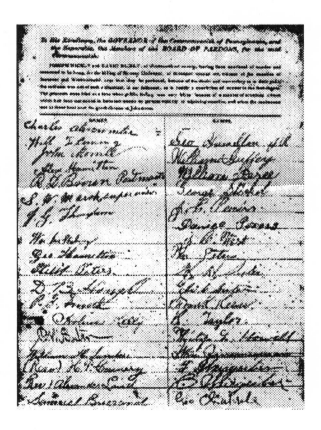

A typical letter sample found listed on the microfilm.

Jones and Jones
Manufacturers and Dealers
Machine Shops and Foundry
South Mill Street
Somerset, Pa. Dec. 19th, 1899.

To the Honorable Board of Pardons

Gentlemen:

The sentiment of the people of Somerset is in favor of the Nicely Boys (now confined in the Somerset Co. jail for the murder of Herman Umberger) so much so that I am convinced that 9/10 of the population are in favor of commutation of sentence.

Respectfully,

J. A. Jones

NOTES

Part One

1. Through discussions with Richard Mayer, former editor of the *Johnstown Democrat* and Richard Burkert, head of JAHA and the Flood Museum, the author learned that his account of "The Morley Dog" is "limited but authentic." Many legends came into being after the flood . . . train engineers, heroic deeds, heroic dogs. There exists a picture of "Romeo"—a large Newfoundland who actually did rescue work—Morley's Dog did not achieve heroic stature until the 1940s when it was donated to the city and placed in a park.

2. Colonel Thomas Cresap of Oldtown, Maryland, was one of the principle agents of the Ohio Company. In 1749 he asked the old Delaware Indian chief, Nemacolin, to show him the best route for a packhorse path between the Potomac River and the headwaters of the Ohio River. The old chief pointed out an Indian trail leading from Will's Creek, now Cumberland, to the Indian towns below the forks of the Ohio River. Christopher Gist, a surveyor from North Carolina, was appointed to search out and discover these lands. The path was adopted as the best route and ever after was known as Nemacolin's Trail (Cassady 1932, 50; cf. Doyle 1945, 18).

3. The Indian mind could conceive little more than immediate revenge against the British for usurping their ancestral lands. Their reasoning revived and intensified their grievances. Into the bloody foray that was to come, there appeared a chieftain believed to be one of the greatest of all Indian warriors. He struck terror in the newly settled people of the territory that would become Somerset County. His name was Pontiac. An Ottawa chieftain, he organized a large resistance that came to be known as Pontiac's War. With the British in command Indian prestige vanished. Pontiac led one last desperate effort to clear the woods of all white men. Throughout the length of the Forbes

Military Road, terror reigned supreme. With the exception of Fort Pitt, Ligonier and Fort Bedford, every British military fort was destroyed. 1763 was indeed a black year for early settlers.

The history of Somerset County would have taken a different turn during the fateful year if a less capable man than Colonel Henry Bouquet had been assigned to command the wilderness campaign against Pontiac. On July 5, Bouquet assembled his army at the foot of the Allegheny Mountains. His forces did not exceed five hundred men of which the most effective were the Scotch Highlanders (Doyle 1945, 32). Contrasting sharply with the Highlanders' bright regalia were the thirty backwoodsmen dressed in buckskins, moccasins and coonskin hats. Bouquet met and defeated Pontiac at Bushy Run on August 5-6, 1763, redeeming the wilderness for the settlers. From a military point of view the lands west of the Alleghenies were now cleared of both French and Indians. November 5, 1768, by Treaty of Fort Stanwix, the land was purchased by the government from the Indians and resold to the settlers. The long vigil of the Indian watch was over. The forts that dotted the county stood as grim reminders of the taut bow-string of the Iroquois and Delaware (Doyle 1945, 58).

Part Two

1.   A persistent tradition of Juniata Valley tells of a heroic figure called "Captain jack." Shirley Wagoner in her article, "Captain Jack—Man or Myth?", states that several entire books have been written about Captain jack, the earliest in 1873. As a rule, they attempt to portray the period faithfully and, to a greater or lesser degree are true to actual historical events and places. However, from 1748 on, more and more squatters moved into Indian territory. The author states that in some of the material, there is confusion as to who Captain Jack may have been.

The following is a copy of a letter to the governor of the province (Wagoner —, 105).

Fort Louther, June 6, 1755

Sir—Captain Jack has promised his aid in the contemplated attack on Fort Du Quesne. He will march width his Hunters, by a circuitous route and join Braddock. He and his men are dressed in hunting shirts, moccasins, etc. are well armed, and are equally [prepared] regardless of heat and cold. They require no shelter for the night. They ask no pay. If the whole army was composed of such men, there would be no cause for apprehension. I shall be with them in time for duty.

> Yours, &c. George Croghan

If genuine, this would be an extremely important letter. It would be an original source certifying Captain Jack's existence and linking him with General Braddock. Many historians do apparently credit this letter, the existence of the man and the reality of his encounter with General Braddock. However, the historical person accompanying the expedition who has perhaps left the longest written record of his life was George Washington. In his correspondence, journals and diaries much history of the time can be viewed first hand. Unfortunately, no diaries exist for the years 1755–1759. Washington was with Braddock most of his march during the fatal battle. Many of his letters from that period have been preserved. In one letter he wrote, "Arrived here an Indian trader with the Half-King," apparently referring to Croghan an one of his Indian chiefs arriving at Fort Cumberland to join Braddock. There are no references to Captain Jack or anyone like him in the correspondence examined (Wagoner, 108).

Perhaps there was a real Captain Jack whose family was massacred and who swore revenge. Perhaps the rest of the story is completely legendary with various exploits and adventures attaching themselves over the years to a singly figure who seemed to embody the spirit of the early frontier.

Or perhaps he never existed. Perhaps the time called for a hero and the myth developed to fit the need for such a heroic figure. All that can be said for certain is that his existence cannot be proven and a skeptical look should be taken at the claims of those who assert his existence as a historical figure (Wagoner, 118).

2. In the "Colonial Records of North Carolina, 1766–1771," in material collected by William L. Saunders, the author makes reference to the fact that Harmon Husband was a member of the legislature and received many of his ideas concerning government from his distinguished relative, Benjamin Franklin.

3. The association of Jeremiah Sullivan Black and John C. Fremont is an interesting and curious one. Brought together during the James Buchanan presidency when Black served both as attorney general and secretary of state, issues of the time brought them together on common ground. Fremont always believed that, had he been elected president, the influence of his and his wife's large family connections in the South would have done much to prevent the Civil War. During the campaign he had given attention to a plan, which later commended itself to Lincoln, for the gradual abolition of slavery with federal compensation, and he had spent some time with Jeremiah S. Black in discussing the details.

Black again was linked with Fremont when he served as his counsel as a result of the fraudulent sale of railroad stocks in France. There was bad misrepresentation. Of the falsehoods circulated in Paris, Fremont knew nothing until later. The episode left an unhappy blemish upon Fremont. It is evident that he had acted with honesty, but it is also certain that he had shown a lamentable lack of discretion (cf. Nevins 1955, II: 457-58; Egan 1977, 443-63).

Part Three

1. The manuscript entitled *Narrative of David Lewis* contains an account of the life and adventures of this celebrated counterfeiter and robber from the commencement of his career until his death in the jail at Belfonte in consequence of a wound received in the attempt by the "Posse Comitatus" of Center County to retake him (Reading Eagle Press, 1928).

2. Herman Umberger's first wife was a half sister of Mrs. A.A. Nicely, the mother of David and Joseph (*Somerset Herald* 1889, 31 May; cf. Doyle 1945, 48).

3. The people of Somerset County had been incensed when on December 16, William F. Weller, another prominent and well-to-do farmer, had been shot. Through he recovered fully from his wound in the course of several weeks, it was generally believed that the motive for the shooting was money. Herman Umberger's murder further incited the indignation of the people (Werner 1890, 6-7).

4. Dr. B.F. Walker, of Jennerstown, made a postmortem examination of Herman Umberger's body. He located two bullet holes, one in the shoulder and another that entered between the seventh and eighth ribs, penetrating the heart (Werner 1890, 6).

5. The following served as jurors in the Nicely brothers' murder trial: E.D. Miller, merchant, of Rockwood; Josiah Newman, farmer, of Summit township; Isaac T. Manges, farmer, of Paint township; Fred F. Walker, farmer, of Summit township; J.W. Beck, farmer, of Southhampton township; J.H. Hite, farmer, of Stoyestown; W.W. Davis, butcher, of Somerset; David J. Wolfersberger, carpenter, of Rockwood; Jeremiah Henry, farmer, Quemahoning township; T.M. Black, clerk, of Confluence; C.W. Weigle, farmer, of Quemahoning township; and Adam J. Sembower, farmer, of Lower Turkeyfoot township (Werner 1890, 20).

6. Dr. Orth's report:

> Joe Nicely moved in a seemingly methodical manner around the rear of the cell, starting from the washstand, which he would seize hold of, shake and pound, then to the smooth wall, passing his right hand along the surface until it met the projecting rib, which he would fumble a short time, then to the corner of the room, where he would pass his fingers over the rivet heads and up and down the angle iron, then pass on to the side and along the wall to another projecting rib, go through the same maneuvers with the same hand. Then, with his left hand and arm continually moving up and down in an aimless way, he would cross the

129

room and repeat his walk, as if seeking some starting point to work his way through the walls. He never approached the cell bars. Noise in the corridors did not apparently in any way attract him (Werner 1890, 71).

7. A chair at the end of an oscillating plank into which scolds or dishonest tradesmen were tied and dunked in water as a punishment.

8. Ira F. Brant, who resided on the Star Route between Ligonier and Stahlstown, Pennsylvania, was an uncle by marriage of the author. In an interview with the author in the spring of 1969, he expressed strong feelings concerning Joseph Nicely. Mr. Brant stated that he had been about four-years-old at the time of the Nicely brothers' murder trial. He remembered going to bed at night and crying because he could not believe that Joseph Nicely was in jail. He remembered Joseph's fine voice, singing in the choir, and a dream in which he saw Joseph ascending to heaven.

9. Joseph Nicely's letter:

Somerset, Pa.
April 2, 1891.

    Dear Wife and Children:
        Oh, how I would like to have seen you and talked to you. Now, Harriet, I want you to be sure and live close to God. Each evening and morning read a chapter from God's Holy Word, and pray with the children; for all you do, do not neglect this and have the children kneel down at their bedside and pray each evening. Oh, live close to the Lord the few years you have to live here.
        My watch I give to Renz, my shot-gun to Ira, my truck and rifle to Waltie. The rifle which Fred Randkin has, sell to him if you can; it ought to bring $10, but if you cannot get that much sell it for less. My books, Lottie gets first choice, Millie second choice, Georgia third choice and Ella fourth. Then begin with Renz and go down to Ella until all are taken. Now

Renz, you and Ira work for your Mother and above all things give your heart to God in your youthful days. Do not put this off. My valise Sheriff Good will send to you.

Sheriff McMillen has in his possession my diary. It will be of a great deal of use to you. Write to him and get it. My diary is in a passbook and a part on sheets of paper. I could have talked to you much better but I pray that God will be with you and keep you faithful to death and at last receive you all to Himself is my prayer.

Your Husband,
J.G. Nicely

10. According to the April 2, 1891 *Somerset Standard*, Sheriff Good received the following telegram on March 28, 1891:

"Elk Lick, Pa. March 27. Sheriff Good. Be on watch tonight. Parties on way to release Nicelys."

The sheriff reportedly read the letter, smiled, and declared his intention to go to bed and take a good night's rest. Yet the belief that the brothers would yet be freed grew in intensity up until almost the very last hour.

11. In his pamphlet *The Umberger Tragedy*, Edward H. Werner sets the Nicely brothers' time of death at 1:37 P.M.

12. Information furnished by Mr. and Mrs. George W. Nicely, Johnstown, Pennsylvania. George Nicely is a son of the Reverend Emerson Lorenzo Nicely and the grandson of Joseph Nicely.

Epilogue

1. Elder Hanawalt conducted the worship service with the benediction given by C. W. Miller. Both were associated with the Dunkard Church (*Greensburg Daily Tribune* 1891, 1 April).

2. Copies of this issue are extant. The rare copies are treasured by many residents of Somerset County.

3. One of the affidavits submitted to the pardon board on March 23, 1891, was that of J. W. Beck, who confirmed that he had been forced by his fellow jurors to agree to a verdict of murder.

4. Anthony Nicely, born 1827, married Elizabeth James, daughter of Daniel James (Old Zion Lutheran Church records).

5. Dr. Orth was head of the State Insane Asylum in Harrisburg and believed to be a close friend of Governor Pattison (*Somerset Herald* 1891, 1 April).

6. Joseph Nicely's prison diary was given to the Somerset County Historical Society by Fadra Richard on 22 August 1988.

7. The "E" is clear. The other letter may be either a "G" or a "C."

8. Judge Robert Ralston was a lawyer and essayist for a quarter of a century who was identified with the Philadelphia bar. He was admitted to the bar in 1885. Soon proving his worth as a counselor and advocate by the wise and conscientious use of his talents, he became known as an attorney of marked devotion to the interests of his clients and yet he was very aware that he owed a higher allegiance to the majesty of the law. In 1892, he was appointed assistant United States district attorney and remained as the incumbent in that office until 1898. His work manifested a notable faculty for the separation of the important features of any subject from its incidental or accidental circumstances (cf. Oberholtzer, 390-91).

Ralston provided an alphabetical list of private or county jail executions. His method of indexing was to include an "R" referring to the study itself, and a page number followed by a hyphen and case number. Thus, the reference to Joseph and David Nicely in Ralston's study is R3-82. Ralston added a notation along with the names of the brothers. "Umberger was a co-conspirator rather than a victim. This should be checked" (cf. Koontz and Welflag 1906, II: 29; Teeters 1961).

9. There is some question as to whether or not the buffalo came as far east as the Allegheny Mountains. Records show that they did.

Sometime before, a Captain Andrew Friend and James Spencer had settled in the Turkeyfoot region. Before the Revolutionary War, while out hunting, they discovered a herd of eight or ten buffalo on the other side of the Casselman River. They managed to shoot a fine, fat one, but the rest escaped. This was the last buffalo killed and the last herd seen in what is now Somerset County (Cassady 1932, 23–24).

10. The friend was Isaac Cox, an early settler.

REFERENCES

American Indian Myths and Legends. Selected and edited by Richard Endors and Alfonso Ortz. New York: Pantheon Books, 1984.

Andrews, Wayne, Editor. *Concise Dictionary of American History*. New York: Charles Scribner's Sons, 1962.

Baker, Carlos. *Emerson Among the Eccentrics*. New York: Viking, Penguin Books, 1996.

Baldwin, N. Leroy. *Two Hundred Years in Shade Township*. Somerset County, 1762-1962, Central City, Pa.: N. Leroy Baldwin, 1964.

The Berlin Record. Berlin, Pa.: 13 December–16 December 1932.

Biographical Dictionary of the American Congress. 1774-1927. United States Government Printing Office. 1928.

Blackburn, E. Howard and William H. Wilfley. *History of Bedford and Somerset County, Pennsylvania*. New York: The Lewis Publishing Co., 1906.

Botkin, B. A. *A Treasury of American Folklore*. New York: Bonanza Books, 1983.

Brigance, William Norwood. *Jeremiah Sullivan Black. A Defense of the Constitution and the Ten Commandments*. New York: Humphry Milfrid, Oxford University Press, 1934.

Buck, Solon J. and Elizabeth Hawthorne Buck. *The Planting of Civilization in Western Pennsylvania*. University of Pittsburgh Press, 1979.

Burt, Olive Wrolley. *American Murder Ballads*. New York: Oxford University Press, 1959.

Cassady, John C. *The Somerset County Outline*. Scottdale, Pa.: Mennonite Publishing House, 1932.

Clayton, Mary Black. *Reminiscences of Jeremiah Sullivan Black*. St. Louis, Mo.: Christian Publishing House, 1897.

Coffin, Tristram Potter and Henning Cohen. *The Parade of Heroes, Legendary Figures in American Lore*. Garden City, New York: Anchor Press, Doubleday, 1978.

Coleman, William H. *The Old Glade Road*. McKeesport, Pa.: October 28, 1941.

"The Conquest of North America." *The Encyclopedia of Discovery and Exploration*. Garden City, New York: Doubleday and Company, Inc., 1971.

Department of Justice, Board of Pardons, Harrisburg, Pa. Microfilm RG15/457. February 1890– March 1893.

Dictionary of American History. Revised Edition, Vol. III. Federal Communicative Commission Job Core. New York: Charles Scribner's Sons, 1976.

Dodcharles, Frederic A. *Daily Stories of Pennsylvania*. Milton, Pa., 1924.

Doncaster, William Trall, Jr. "The Right Hand of David 'Robber' Lewis," *Historical and Genealogical Society of Somerset County*, "Laurel Messenger," Vol. 26, No. 3, August, 1985.

Dorson, Richard M. *American Folklore*. The University of Chicago Press, 1967.

Doyle, Frederic. *Early Somerset County*. Somerset, Pa.: Somerset County Historical Society, 1945.

Drago, Harry Sinclair. *Road Agents and Train Robbers*. New York: Dodd, Mead and Company, 1973.

"Early Somerset County History." Somerset, Pa.: Somerset Chamber of Commerce.

Echart, Alan W. *Wilderness Empire*. Boston, Mass.: Little Brown and Company, 1969.

Egan, Ferol. *Fremont-Explorer for a Restless Nation*. Garden City, New York: Doubleday and Company, Inc., 1977.

Emrich, Duncan. *Folklore on the American Land*. Boston, Mass.: Little, Brown and Company, 1972.

Endors, Richard and Ortz, editors. *American Myths and Legends*. New York: Pantheon Books, 1984.

Ehrheart, R. C. "American Folklore," *Somerset Democrat*. Somerset, Pa. December 11, 1962.

Fletcher, Stevenson Whitcomb. *Pennsylvania Agriculture and Country Life, 1640-1840*. Harrisburg, Pa.: Commonwealth of Pennsylvania, Pennsylvania Historical and Museum Commission, 1971.

Frazer, Ellis Wilson. *Arthur St. Clair, Rugged Ruler of the Old Northwest, An American Epic of the Old Frontier*. Garrett and Massie, 1944.

Graymore, Barbara, *The Iroquois in the American Revolution*. Syracuse University Press, 1972.

Greensburg Daily Tribune. Greensburg, Pa. 23 March–7 April 1891.

Greensburg Morning Review. Greensburg, Pa. 7 July 1974.

Hall, William M. *Reminiscences and Sketches, Historical and Biographical, Meyers Printing House*, Harrisburg, Pa. 1890.

Henry, Thomas R. *Wilderness Messiah, The Story of Hiawatha and the Iroquois*. New York: William Sloan Associates, 1955.

History of Bedford. Somerset and Fulton Counties, Pennsylvania. Chicago: Waltermann, Watkins and Co., 1884.

Hunter, William A. *John Badollett's Journal of the Time I Spent in the Stoney Creek Glades, 1793-1794*, Vol. CIV, April 1982. *The Pennsylvania Magazine of History and Biography*.

Jardon, Andre. *Tocqueville, A Biography*. translated from the French by Lydia Davis with Robert Hemeney. Farrar, Straus and Girous, 1988.

Jones, J. J. *History of the Early Settlement of Juniata Valley*. With notes and extensions compiled as a glossary from the memoirs of early settlers, the pension statements of Revolutionary War soldiers and other source material as edited by Floyd G. Hoenstine. Harrisburg, Pa.: *The Telegraph Press*, 1940.

Kane, Joseph Nathan. *Famous First Facts*. New York: H. W. Wilson, 1950, i.e., 1954.

Koestler, Arthur. *The Trial of the Dinosaur-Reflections on Hanging*. The Danube Edition, Hutchison of London, 1970.

Koontz, William H., Editor. *History of Bedford and Somerset Counties, Pennsylvania*. Bedford County by E. Howard Blackburn, Somerset County by William H. Welfley. New York: The Lewis Publishing Company, 1906.

Korson, George Gershon. *Pennsylvania Songs and Legends*. Philadelphia, Pa.: University of Pennsylvania Press, 1949.

Langsdale, Franklin J. *The Story of a Mountain Railroad*. Reprinted from the original book by means of a photographic process with the full consent of the owner of the copyright, Mrs. Mabel T. Langsdale.

Lathrop, Elsie. *Early Inns and Taverns*. New York: Tudor Publishing Company, 1935.

"Laurel Messenger" in *Historical and Genealogical Society of Somerset County,* Vol. 32, No. 2. May 2, 1991.

Martin, Richard. *Bulfinch's Mythology*. New York: Harper Collins, 1991.

Matthews, Wayne. *Concise Dictionary of American People*. New York: Charles Scribner's Sons, 1952.

McClure, Alex K. *Old Time Notes of Pennsylvania*. Philadelphia, Pa.: The John C. Winston Company, 1905.

McCullough, David G. *The Johnstown Flood*. New York: Simon and Schuster, 1968. Selected references.

McDade, Thomas M. *The Annals of Murder*. University of Oklahoma Press, 1961.

McMasters, John B. *History of the People of the United States,* Vol. I. Appleton, 1927.

Nevins, Allan. *Fremont, Pathmaker of the West*. Vol II. New York: Frederick Ungar Publishing Company, 1955.

Newman, Graeme. *The Punishment Reforms- School of Criminal Justice*. State University of New York at Albany. Philadelphia, Pa.: P. Lippincott Company, 1978.

Nicely, Joseph, Diary. Somerset County Historical Museum. Somerset, Pa., 16 September 1889–18 March 1890.

Oberholtzer, Ellis Paxson. *Philadelphia—A History of the City and Its People*. Vol. IV. Philadelphia, Pa.: The S. J. Clarke Publishing Co.

Pennsylvania Folklore Society, Vol. I. No. 4. "Two Pennsylvania Mountain Legends." Collected by Henry W. Shoemaker. Reading, Pa.: Reading Eagle Press, 1928.

Pletcher, Russ. "1700s: When Buffalo Roamed the Mountains." *Visitor's Quarterly-Winter,* '94-95. Somerset, Pa.: Jeff O'Brien, Publisher.

Ralston, Robert. *Delay in Execution of Murderers.* Pennsylvania Bar Association, 1911.

Rial, David W. "The Old Forbes Road." *Carnegie Magazine.* February 1954.

Robinson, Felix G. "The Frosty Sons of Thunder." *Tableland Trails,* Vol I. No 2, Summer, 1953.

Shank, William H. *Indian Trail to Super Highway.* York, Pa.: American Canal and Transportation Center, 1967.

Shank, William H. *Indian Trail to Super Highway.* 2d ed. York, Pa.: American Canal and Transportation Center, 1988.

Shank, William H. *Vanderbilt's Folly, A History of the Pennsylvania Turnpike.* York, Pa.: American Central and Transportation Center, 1973.

Shoemaker, Henry W. *Two Pennsylvania Mountain Legends.* Reading, Pa.: Reading Eagle Press, 1928.

Shoemaker, Henry W. and John Joseph McVey. *Juniata Memories.* Philadelphia, Pa., 1916.

Singmaster, Elsie. *Stories of Pennsylvania,* Vol. III, 1787–1830. The Pennsylvania Book Series. Harrisburg, Pa., 1938.

Sipe, C. Hale. "Fort Ligonier and Its Times." *The Telegraph Press.* Harrisburg, Pa., 1932.

Sobel, Robert and John Rarne, Editors. *Biographical Dictionary of the Governors of the United States, 1889-1978.* United States Government Printing Office, 1928.

Somerset American. Somerset, Pa. March 15, 1979.

Somerset Democrat. Somerset, Pa. April 1, 1891.

Somerset Herald. Somerset, Pa. 31 May–8 June 1889.

Somerset Herald. Somerset, Pa. 1 April–8 April 1891.

Somerset Standard. Somerset, Pa. 3 April 3–10 April 1891.

Somerset County. Pennsylvania, Somerset Chamber of Commerce. Somerset, Pa., no date.

Studer, Gerald C. "Frederich Goeb, Master Printer." *Goeb Bible Sesquicentennial, Somerset,* Pa. October, 1963.

Tableland Trails, Vol. 1 No. 2. Summer 1953.

Tales of Pioneer Pittsburgh. American Guild Series. Material gathered and written by the Pittsburgh Unit of the Federal Writer's Project in Pennsylvania. Published by the William Penn Association, 1937.

Terrell, John Upton. *American Indian Almanac.* New York: The World Publishing Co., 1971.

Teeters, Negley K. *Scaffold and Chair, Compilation of Their Use in Pennsylvania From 1682 to 1962.* Sponsored by the Pennsylvania Prison Society of Pennsylvania, Lancaster County Historical Society, 1963.

Teeters, Negley K. "Tentative List of Hangings in County Jails of Pennsylvania, 1834-1913." Professor of Sociology, Temple University, Philadelphia. Spring 1961.

Trombley, Stephen. *The Execution Protocol, Inside American Capitol Punishment Industry.* New York: Crown Publishers, Inc., 1992.

"Turning Back Through the Pages of History." The *Berlin Record,* Berlin, Pennsylvania. 13 December–16 December 1932.

Twentieth Century Bench and Bar of Pennsylvania, Vol. I and II. Chicago: H. C. Cooper Company, Jr. Bro. and Co., 1903.

Vogt, Helen. *Westward Of Ye Laurel Hills, 1750-1850.* Parsons, West Va.: McClain Printing Company, 1976.

Wagoner, Shirley A. "Captain Jack—Man or Myth?" *Pennsylvania History.* Dallas, Pa.: The Pennsylvania Historical Society, Payne Printers, Inc.

Walkinshaw, L.C. *Annals of Southwestern Pennsylvania.* New York: Lewis Historical Publishing Company, Inc., 1939.

Wallace, Paul A. W. *Conrad Weiser, 1696- 1760, Friend of Colonist and Mohawk.* Philadelphia, Pa.: University of Pennsylvania Press, 1945.

Wallace, Paul A. W. *Pennsylvania, Seed of a Nation.* New York: Harper and Row, 1962.

Walton, Walter F. "The South Pennsylvania Railroad" or "The Road That Might Have Been." History and Heritage Committee, Pittsburgh Section, American Society of Engineers, 1982.

Werner, Edward H. *The Umberger Tragedy.* Somerset, Pa.: Printed in the office of *The Highland Farmer,* 1890.

Whisher, Vaughn. "Tales of the Allegheny Foothills." *Bedford Gazette,* Bedford, Pa. 11 June 1978.

Ziukas, Tim. "Rebellious Spirits." *The Pittsburgh Gazette.* April 17, 1994.

139

About the Author

William Trall Doncaster, Jr., was born in Greensburg, Pennsylvania, just weeks preceding the end of World War I. The son of Dr. William Trall Doncaster, Sr. and Jane Miller Doncaster, he grew up in an atmosphere of medical terms and practices, the third generation of physicians, the mantle of which fell to his brother Richard. With a great respect for, but no inclination towards medicine, his early interest was history and the humanities, inspired by his paternal grandfather, Dr. William Hess Doncaster, whose renowned eclecticism was to become a part of his heritage. Following an undergraduate degree in history, with an absorbing interest in the scholastics and the piety of the monks of the Middle Ages, he pursued a Master's degree in Theology at the Princeton Theological Seminary.

During his early ministry, he continued his studies in history to complete his Doctorate of Philosophy degree at the University of Pittsburgh. He served as pastor of three Presbyterian churches in southwestern Pennsylvania, all within the lengthening shadow of the Allegheny Mountains, whose legends would one day become one of his great interests, and the content of this book.

Dr. Doncaster enjoyed a forty-three year residency in Somerset, Pennsylvania, and a forty year marriage to Marjorie Walker Doncaster, piano teacher of the classical school, and photographer, distinguished in both fields. Her music has been published by Belwin Banner Books and her photography has been exhibited at the Carnegie Museum in Pittsburgh where she received numerous awards. The Doncasters have one daughter, Debra Doncaster Bruce, married to Samuel G. Bruce, Jr., of Richmond, Virginia, and two grandchildren, Lauren and Adam.